MATHS

The Wacky Way

For Students...By A Student

Claire Gallagher

AuthorHouse™ UK Ltd.
500 Avebury Boulevard
Central Milton Keynes, MK9 2BE
www.authorhouse.co.uk
Phone: 08001974150

First published by AuthorHouse   6/15/2009

ISBN: 978-1-4389-3989-6 (sc)

Printed in the United States of America
Bloomington, Indiana

This book is printed on acid-free paper.

authorHOUSE®

Acknowledgements

This book has been so long in coming to completion, I have lots of people to mention.

To everyone I have tutored over the years: Hannah, Dom, Craig, Ross, Sarah, Cara, Harry, Charlotte, Liam, Alex, Claire, Kimberly, Tash, Emily, Martin, Pamela, Nigella, Lexie, Sophie and Mark, to mention but a few of the many, without their great exam success this would not have been possible.

A particular thanks goes to my A Level Maths teacher, Malcolm, for recommending me to new students over the years and keeping me updated with any changes to the Maths syllabus.

A special thanks goes to Julie, Steph and David without whose help and support I could not have got the book finally ready for publishing.

To all my friends, for their understanding over the years, for not being available for socialising, a situation I now intend to rectify!

A big thanks to Dave for being so patient with the final checks.

Finally, to my family, especially my parents and Grandma for always supporting and encouraging me.

Sections shown in **red** are only on the higher level GCSE Maths paper
Sections in **black and red** have some areas that are on the higher level paper.

This is according to the main exam boards

Contents

Section 1 – The Fundamentals

Terminology

Before you get started with the book, make sure you are happy with the following words and their meanings:

Integers

An integer is a whole number, it is not a fraction or a decimal.

Multiples

Multiples are the numbers that appear in a times table, so multiples of 3 are the numbers that appear in the 3 times tables.

Factors

Factors are integers that divide into a number to leave an integer. It is also the times tables which the number appears in.

For example:

If asked for factors of 72, consider which times tables the number 72 appears in.

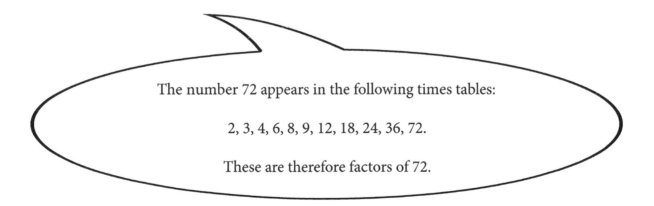

The number 72 appears in the following times tables:

2, 3, 4, 6, 8, 9, 12, 18, 24, 36, 72.

These are therefore factors of 72.

Lowest/Highest Common Factor

If asked for the lowest common factor of two numbers, find the factors for both numbers then take the lowest factor that appears for both numbers.

If asked for the highest common factor of two numbers, find the factors for both numbers then take the highest factor that appears for both numbers.

Prime Numbers

A prime number is a number that can only be divided by itself and one. However, the number one is not a prime number.

For example:

2, 3, 5, 7, 11, 13, 17, etc.

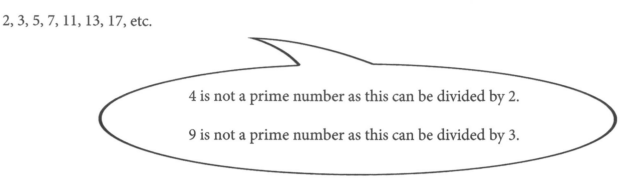

4 is not a prime number as this can be divided by 2.

9 is not a prime number as this can be divided by 3.

Powers

Powers are used in order to simplify sums. Instead of writing 2 x 2 x 2 x 2, this can be written as 2^4. Where a number is multiplied by itself the number of times can be written as a power.

For example:

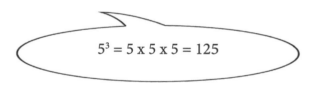

$5^3 = 5 \times 5 \times 5 = 125$

Roots

This is effectively going backwards, so if you wanted to find what number multiplied by itself so many times gives an answer, you would use a root.

For example:

$\sqrt[3]{125} = 5$

This is asking you to find the number which multiplied by itself five times equals 125

Now try these:

1. What are factors of 96?

2. List multiples of 7

3. Find the highest common factor of 18 and 54

4. Find the highest common factor of 33 and 18

5. What is $\sqrt[3]{64}$?

6. What is 2^5 ?

Negative Numbers

Think of your age, how many pets you have or the house number you live at. You say these numbers and never mention the positive, so we assume unless otherwise stated that numbers are positive.

If a number is a negative the number has a minus in front of it.

If there are two negatives next to each other, the minus and the minus come together to make a plus as shown below:

If you multiply or divide two negative numbers, the same rules apply. A minus and a minus make a plus.

Where there are one of each sign, the positive is ignored so it is the minus that is left behind. You could think of it as the minus needs another minus there to change it into a positive. The minus will remain if it's on its own.

When you multiply or divide numbers, do the multiplication or division first and then look at the signs.

For example:

-3 x -12

 = 36

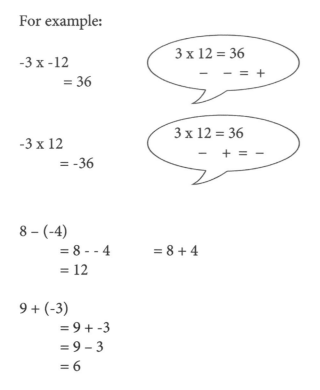

3 x 12 = 36

–   – = +

-3 x 12

 = -36

3 x 12 = 36

–   + = –

8 – (-4)

 = 8 - - 4   = 8 + 4

 = 12

9 + (-3)

 = 9 + -3

 = 9 – 3

 = 6

Sometimes counting with negative numbers can cause confusion, especially if you are unable to use a calculator.

For example:

$-2 + (-8) = ?$

As mentioned previously, you already know that this is exactly the same as $-2 - 8$. If you find the negative confusing, think of the negative numbers as being below ground level. If you are already below ground by 2 and takeaway 8, you will be underground by 10 (-10).

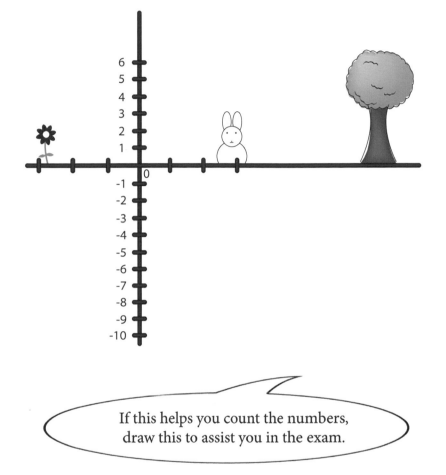

If this helps you count the numbers,
draw this to assist you in the exam.

You are below ground level if there is a negative number. If you are already below ground by 2, you are going to go down a further 8 so will end up below ground by 10.

If you were given a negative number firstly but then you are adding a number to this amount, you will be heading towards the surface.

For example:

$-9 + 5 = ?$

You are already below ground by 9 but you are going to travel up 5 so you will now only be below ground by 4. (Answer = -4)

Now try these:

1. -4 x 7 = ?

2. 50 ÷ -5 = ?

3. 16 + (-19) = ?

4. 5 – (-8) = ?

Rounding

This is an extremely important area as on a calculator paper you may be asked to round in a certain way. You will need to do this in order to gain full marks. If they don't tell you what to round to, you can round at the end of the question but put in brackets what you have rounded to.

Decimal Places

When rounding to decimal places, the number of decimal places that you round to is how many will be shown. It is possible that the last number may change if it is followed by a five or above. If this is the case it will increase by one, but be careful if the last number shown is a nine and it is followed by a five or higher.

For example:

3.43582 would be 3.44 to 2dp, 3.436 to 3dp, 3.4358 to 4dp, etc.

Significant Figures

This is another way of rounding, however counting starts from the first number. If the number you stop on is followed by a five or higher, you also need to increase the number by one.

For example:

3.43582 would be 3.44 to 3sf, 3.436 to 4sf, etc.

There are some additional points that should be noted.

If the number is very small, there may be zeros in the number at the beginning. If you were to round to decimal places these numbers may not appear as any number.

For example:

0.00005687 to 3dp is 0.000

With significant figures (sf) it is helpful to think of these numbers as big inflatable numbers in a bouncy castle.

You would start counting from the first 'real' numbers i.e. zeros at the beginning will not count.

If you imagine having a row of inflatable numbers, you knock the numbers over if they are zeros until you hit a non zero. This is when you would start counting, however the zeros that were knocked down will pop back up into place.

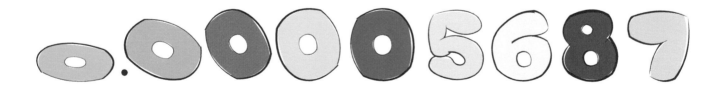

For example:

0.00005687 to 3sf is 0.0000569

When you have an integer the rounding is the same. You would count from the beginning of the number but then look at what the number is that you have landed on. For example a ten, a hundred, a thousand, etc. You then need to round to the nearest ten, hundred or thousand, whichever is applicable.

For example:

53,453 to 3sf is 53,500 because the third number is a hundred so you would need to round to the nearest hundred.

Now try these:

1. Round the following to 3dp:

a) 23.6132
b) 2.05108
c) 8.60989

2. Round the following to 3sf:

a) 0.00029862
b) 89,785
c) 85.36189

Estimations

To receive full marks there is a certain way you will need to estimate.

You should round the number to one significant figure. By doing this it will be easy to work out the answer without the calculator.

For example:

$$\text{Estimate} \quad \frac{367 \times 9801}{78}$$

$$= \frac{400 \times 10,000}{80}$$

$$= \frac{4,000,000}{80}$$

$$= 50,000$$

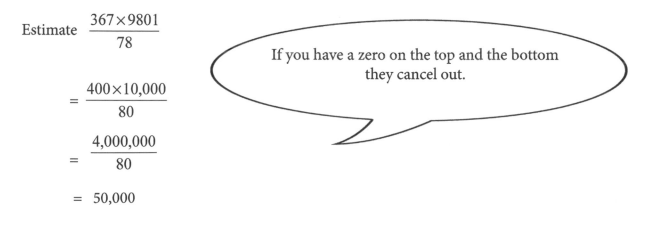

If you have a zero on the top and the bottom they cancel out.

Now try these:

1. Estimate $\dfrac{23 \times 6{,}453}{31}$

2. Estimate $\dfrac{2{,}877 \times 62}{12}$

3. Estimate $\dfrac{324 \times 979}{0.23}$

Simplifying Expressions

You may be asked a question which asks you to simplify an expression, or it could be that you need to do it at the end as part of a bigger question. This is important as there could be several marks for this on a paper.

If you are given an algebraic expression you need to gather terms together, this is what simplifying means. If the expression has different unknowns then they will not be put together. Different unknowns could be x, y, x^2, y^3, z, etc.

It is helpful to think of these questions as if they are objects. If you think of each of the unknowns as an object you can just add up the 'objects'.

For example:

Simplify $5x - 2x + 3x - x$

You need to think of each x as an apple on a shopping list.

You could say you need to get 5 apples, take away 2 apples, add another 3 apples and take off one apple.

How many apples do you have?   5 apples ($5x$)

If there are other unknowns in the expression you must keep them separate.

For example:

Simplify $6y + 5x - 2y + x$

You can now introduce y as being a banana. You need to get 6 bananas and 5 apples, take away 2 of the bananas and add another apple.

What do you have? $4y + 6x$

You may be asked to expand or factorise expressions.

To factorise generally means to put at least one bracket into the expressions. Take the value that appears in all parts of the expression outside of a bracket as this can then be multiplied by the bracket in order to get back to the original expression.
For example:

Factorise $2x + 8$
$\qquad = 2(x + 4)$

The number 2 goes into both $2x$ and 8 so take this outside the bracket. You can then put the values that would be required to get back to the original expression in the inside of the bracket.

To expand means to remove the brackets by expanding the expression. If the bracket has been placed next to the number, this will multiply the contents of the bracket.

For example:

Expand $6(t - 5)$
$\qquad = 6t - 30$

The 6 is multiplied by the 't' and then the '$- 5$' in turn to remove the brackets.

Now try these:

1. Simplify:

   a) $5x + 7y - 3y + x$

   b) $t^2 + 6t + 5t^2 - 2t$

   c) $2g^3 + 8g^2 - 7g - 5g^2 + 3g$

2. Factorise:

   a) $4y + 20$

   b) $3x^2 + 9x$

   c) $5xy + 15x^2 - 10xy^2$

3. Expand:

   a) $9(t + 5)$

   b) $2f(3 - g)$

   c) $3y(x + 6 - y)$

Solving Equations

When you see the phrase 'solve' you are trying to find an exact value.

For example: Solve $6x + 9 = 81$

It would be very easy for you to input different numbers to see which one works and get the right answer, however you would not get full marks. You should bear in mind that method marks are just as important, if not more important than the correct answer.

You are therefore trying to find a value for x. The general rule is to leave the unknown (x) where it is and move everything else from around it.

In order to find the unknown it is a good idea to think of a popular computer game where you control the characters' lives ensuring that they are sociable, eat, sleep, etc. If you think of the unknown as the character you are controlling, when it is with another character it means that they are talking and therefore boosting their sociability levels. You should therefore leave the 'other characters' next to the unknown as long as possible and not move them until you need to.

If you relate this to an equation, when the unknown is multiplying or dividing it is seen as being with the other character. You therefore need to move anything that is not touching the unknown first.

You need to move everything away from the unknown. Anything that is moved will always move to the other side of the equals sign.

Think of a man sitting in the equals sign, when something crosses him he gives a high five to make it the opposite of what it was. So when it changes side, it also changes sign. The sign becomes the opposite of what it was, so a multiplication will become a division. An addition will become subtraction, squared becomes square rooted, etc.

When other figures are moved you should ensure that they do not 'jump the queue' when going to the other side. They will always join the back of the line.

For example: $6x + 9 = 81$

The aim is to get x on its own as it is the unknown

The 6 is 'talking' to it so you should move this last, therefore you need to move the 9. At the moment the 9 is adding, this means it needs to move to the other side and become subtraction.

$$6x = 81 - 9$$

By simplifying this we get $6x = 72$

The next step is to move the 6 which is currently multiplying the x, so it will go to the other side and become a division.

$$x = 72 \div 6$$

By simplifying, the result is $x = 12$. This makes sense because putting 12 back into the equation does equal 81.

For example:

Solve $5y - 12 = 28$

$5y = 28 + 12$
$5y = 40$
$y = 40 \div 5$
$y = 8$

Solve $t^2 + 7 = 43$

$t^2 = 43 - 7$
$t^2 = 36$
$t = \sqrt{36}$
$t = 6$

There is an exception to the rule as when the unknown is not on the same level as the rest of the equation (it is dividing). An example of this is when it is on the bottom of the fraction:

$$9 = \frac{27}{x}$$

You then need to think of our character as not being on ground level, she is hanging off a cliff. This means she needs to move first before anyone else to get her to safety.

She is currently dividing the 27, so she will go to the other side, get a high five by the man in the equals sign and become a multiplication.

$$9 \text{ x } x = 27$$
$$9x = 27$$

The 9 can now move away from the unknown. The 9 is currently multiplying so it will go to the other side and become a division.

$$x = 27 \div 9$$
$$x = 3$$

However there is another exception to this rule, as you could be given the following equation:

$$\frac{3}{x} + 7 = 19$$

If this was the case you have somebody hanging off the cliff but someone standing on their own on the same side. If this is the case you need to get rid of the person standing on their own as they can go and get help. They therefore move to the other side first, then you can move the person hanging off the cliff.

For example:

$$\frac{3}{x} + 7 = 19$$

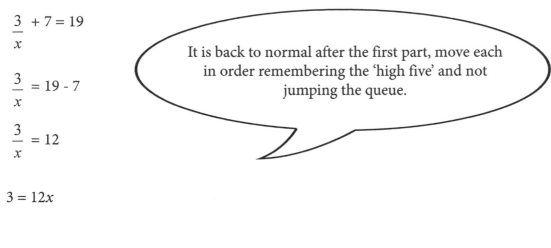

It is back to normal after the first part, move each in order remembering the 'high five' and not jumping the queue.

$$\frac{3}{x} = 19 - 7$$

$$\frac{3}{x} = 12$$

$$3 = 12x$$

$$x = 3/12$$

$$x = 0.25$$

Hopefully you are now happy with the one unknown but what happens if the unknown appears more than once?

For example:

$$8x + 3 = 3x + 13$$

If this is the case, think of the x as being our person but the number next to it as representing how many pies have been eaten.

In the example there would have been eight pies on one side and three pies on the other side.

The side that has the most pies is the heaviest and therefore that person will stay where they are. The other pies will move to this side and all the integers to the opposite side. You can then 'tidy up' and get the unknown on its own.

For example:

$$12t - 4 = 8t + 36$$
$$12t - 8t = 36 + 4$$
$$4t = 40$$
$$t = \frac{40}{4}$$
$$t = 10$$

Now try these:

1. Solve $5x + 3 = 28$

2. Solve $7y - 9 = 3y + 27$

3. Solve $\dfrac{t}{3} + 7 = 11$

Indices

Indices are powers, for example ^{3} or ^{2}. You may be asked to multiply or divide numbers in index form. If you have questions with indices, look to see if the numbers are on the same level as the multiplication or division sign.

When multiplying or dividing, pretend it is really windy so the signs get blown around.

The multiplication sign goes up in the air to join the higher numbers but it is windy and it twists to become a plus. Therefore, you need to add the powers.

$$V^a \quad \text{x} \quad V^b \quad = \quad V^{a+b}$$

When there is a division sign, it goes up in the air to join the numbers at the higher level but it is windy and it loses its dots. Therefore, it becomes a subtraction sign.

$$V^c \quad \div \quad V^d \quad = \quad V^{c-d}$$

For example:

Simplify $y^4 \text{ x } y^5$
            $= y^{4+5} = y^9$

Simplify $j^8 \div j^2$
            $= j^{8-2} = j^6$

Remember: 't' is t^1, hence why t^2 x $t = t^3$

Simplify $t^2 \text{ x } t$
            $= t^{2+1} = t^3$

When numbers are inserted before the unknowns, you need to look at the different levels.

$$cx^a \text{ x } dx^b = cdx^{a+b}$$

As c and d are on the same level as the multiply, they will be multiplied together. The a and b are the same level as the addition sign so will be added together.

$$gx^e \div hx^f = \frac{g}{h}x^{e-f}$$

As g and h are on the same level as the divide, g will be divided by h. The e and f are the same level as the subtract sign so f will be subtracted from e.

Further examples:

Simplify $5t^3$ x $4t^6$
        $5t^3 \text{ x } 4t^6 = 20t^9$

Simplify $42y^5 \div 7y^2$
        $42y^5 \div 7y^2 = 6y^3$

Now try these:

1. Simplify:

   a) $t^5 \times t^7$
   b) $x^{10} \div x^6$
   c) $g^8 \times g$

2. Simplify:

   a) $6k^2 \times 5k^9$
   b) $32f^8 \div 4f$
   c) $7r^3 \times 3r^6$

Inequalities

Inequalities (symbols like >, ≤, <, etc) will probably appear in these questions so you need to ensure you understand them.

Read the inequality across with your finger. If you touch the larger opening of the inequality you would say greater than but if you touched the small point first it would be less than.

For example:

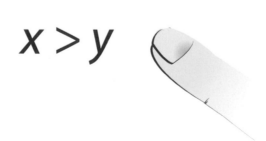

$x > y$

This would be x is greater than y ......

or .... y is less than x (reading across the other way).

$x > y$

$r < t$

This would be r is less than t ....

or .... t is greater than r (reading across the other way).

If the value can also be equal to the amount, a line is placed under the inequality.

For example:

$x \geq y$

This would be x is greater than or equal to y …..

or …… y is less than or equal to x (reading across the other way).

$m \leq p$

This would be m is less than or equal to p …..

or ….. p is greater than or equal to m (reading across the other way).

Solving Inequalities

It is possible to be given an equation which includes an inequality instead of an equals sign. Where this is the case, treat the inequality as if it is an equals sign. The only difference in the treatment is if you multiply or divide a side by a negative, it will then swap the inequality to the opposite side.

For example:

Find possible values of x when $4x + 3 \geq 19$

$4x \geq 19 - 3$
$4x \geq 16$
$x \geq 16 \div 4$
$x \geq 4$

Find possible values of x when $-4x + 3 \geq 19$

$-4x \geq 19 - 3$
$-4x \geq 16$
$x \leq 16 \div -4$
$x \leq -4$

Finding possible values

There are some questions which ask for possible values to fit some ranges. We have previously discussed how you read the inequalities.

For example, if you had the following inequality $1 \leq x < 6$, this means that x is less than 6 (reading across from the x, touching the small point first). Going the other way, x is greater than or equal to one (reading back from the x, touching the larger part first). The possible integers could therefore be 1,2,3,4 or 5.

What if x is not on its own?

For example: $-3 \leq 3x < 12$

If this was a normal equation, you would move the 3 to the other side to leave x on its own. The problem here is that there are two sides. This does not matter, you can divide both the sides by 3 to leave the x on its own. You would therefore get $-1 \leq x < 4$, possible values -1, 0, 1, 2 or 3.

For example:

Find possible values of x when $-1 < 4x - 5 \leq 11$

$$-1 + 5 < 4x \leq 11 + 5$$

$$4 < 4x \leq 16$$

$$4 \div 4 < x \leq 16 \div 4$$

$$1 < x \leq 4$$

Possible integers could be 2, 3 or 4.

Now try these:

1. Find possible values of x when $8x - 9 \geq 23$

2. Find possible values of x when $-3 < 5x + 7 \leq 22$

3. Find possible values of x when $6x - 11 \geq 2x + 13$

4. Find possible values of x when $12 - 8x \geq 60$

Section 2 – Fractions, Percentages & Decimals

Simplifying Fractions

Where possible, always try to simplify your fractions. There are two types of simplifying you may be asked to do.

Top Heavy

Where a fraction has a larger top compared to its bottom, you need to simplify the fraction. If you do not do this it will topple over as the top is bigger than the bottom.

Look at how many times the bottom goes into the top. The amount that is left over goes back into the fraction over the original bottom number.

For example:

$$\frac{39}{7} = 5\frac{4}{7} \qquad\qquad \frac{61}{9} = 6\frac{7}{9}$$

Common factor

If a fraction has a common factor in both the top and bottom of the fraction, this can be taken out to simplify it down.

Where both the top and bottom are even numbers, you are always able to halve both the top and bottom (divide by 2).

For example:

$$\frac{21}{36} \div 3 \rightarrow \frac{7}{12}$$

$$\frac{56}{80} \div 2 \rightarrow \frac{28}{40} \div 2 \rightarrow \frac{14}{20} \div 2 \rightarrow \frac{7}{10}$$

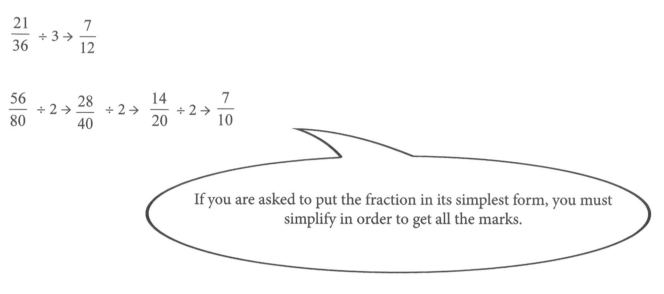

If you are asked to put the fraction in its simplest form, you must simplify in order to get all the marks.

Sums with fractions

No matter what you are doing (addition, division, etc) you need to multiply the fractions either across or diagonally, this will stop you making mistakes. Addition and subtraction of fractions have similar rules as do the multiplication and division of fractions.

Addition and Subtraction of Fractions

When adding and subtracting fractions you need to remember the following dance move:

You multiply diagonally one way, multiply the other diagonal way then straight across the bottom of the fractions.

Addition

$$\frac{A}{B} + \frac{C}{D} = \frac{AD + BC}{BD}$$

For example:

$$\frac{3}{5} + \frac{1}{7} = \frac{21 + 5}{35} = \frac{26}{35}$$

Subtraction

$$\frac{A}{B} - \frac{C}{D} = \frac{AD - BC}{BD}$$

For example:

$$\frac{3}{5} - \frac{1}{7} = \frac{21 - 5}{35} = \frac{16}{35}$$

Multiplication and Division of Fractions

Multiplication

You need to remember the multiplication as being 'happy times'. 'Happy' because they are straight forward. Multiply the tops across then multiply the bottoms across.

$$\frac{A}{B} \times \frac{C}{D} = \frac{AC}{BD}$$

For example:

$$\frac{3}{5} \times \frac{1}{7} = \frac{3}{35}$$

Division

In order to divide you need to change the divide into a multiplication.

If you reverse the division sign into a multiplication sign, you also need to reverse the fraction that follows the division sign. This then changes into the multiplication of two fractions which we saw previously.

$$\frac{A}{B} \div \frac{C}{D} = \frac{A}{B} \times \frac{D}{C} = \frac{AD}{BC}$$

For example:

$$\frac{3}{5} \div \frac{1}{7} = \frac{3}{5} \times \frac{7}{1} = \frac{21}{5} = 4\frac{1}{5}$$

What should you do if the fractions have integers in front of them? Always change the fractions into a top heavy format in order to calculate the sum.

For example:

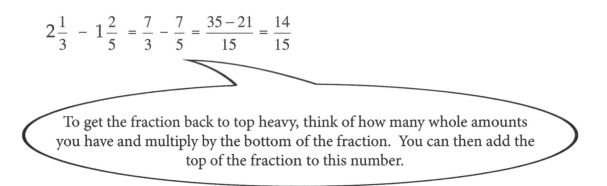

$$2\frac{1}{3} - 1\frac{2}{5} = \frac{7}{3} - \frac{7}{5} = \frac{35-21}{15} = \frac{14}{15}$$

To get the fraction back to top heavy, think of how many whole amounts you have and multiply by the bottom of the fraction. You can then add the top of the fraction to this number.

Now try these:

1. $\dfrac{7}{11} \div \dfrac{3}{8}$

2. $\dfrac{6}{7} + \dfrac{9}{10}$

3. $\dfrac{11}{12} - \dfrac{4}{5}$

4. $5\dfrac{1}{2} - 1\dfrac{4}{5}$

5. $2\dfrac{1}{4} + 3\dfrac{2}{3}$

Finding a Percentage

You may be asked a question on the non calculator paper which asks you to find a percentage. In order to do this .....

$10\% = \dfrac{1}{10}$ Divide number by 10

$20\% = \dfrac{1}{5}$ Divide number by 5

$25\% = \dfrac{1}{4}$ Divide number by 4

$50\% = \dfrac{1}{2}$ Divide number by 2

$5\% = \dfrac{1}{20}$ Divide number by 10 and then 2

$1\% = \dfrac{1}{100}$ Divide number by 10 and then 10 again

Or, if you are given a percentage to find you can break this down into 10%s and 1%s.

For example:

Find 32% of £320

10% = £32.00
 1% = £ 3.20

3 x £32   = £96.00
2 x £3.20 = £6.40
          £102.40

Another commonly tested percentage question includes VAT at the rate of 17.5%.

In order to find the VAT of an amount the percentage should be broken down. Instead of trying to find 17.5%, it should be broken down as follows:

10%
5%
2.5%

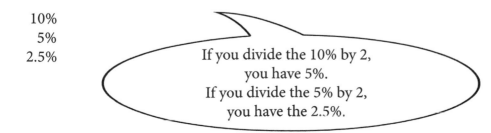

If you divide the 10% by 2, you have 5%.
If you divide the 5% by 2, you have the 2.5%.

For example:

Find 17.5% of £320

10%	= £32
5%	= £16
2.5%	= £ 8
	£56

17.5% is therefore £56

Now try these (without a calculator):

1. If a sofa costs £600 excluding VAT, what would the price be including VAT @17.5%?

2. If there is a 35% sale what would a washing machine cost in the sale if it was originally sold at £250?

3. If you are entitled to 24% of a lottery win of £63,000, how much would you receive?

Changing Percentage, Decimals and Fractions

This is a very popular area for the examiners to test.

Changing a percentage into a decimal

To change a percentage into a decimal you need to divide the percentage by 100. If you divide the percentage by 100 you are effectively moving the decimal point to the left twice.
However, the only thing you need to consider is the following template:

H T U

— . — —

So, if you are given a percentage you need to ask yourself how many hundreds, tens and units are in the number.

For example:

57%	0 hundreds, 5 tens, 7 units	→	0.57
13%	0 hundreds, 1 ten, 3 units	→	0.13
20%	0 hundreds, 2 tens, 0 units	→	0.20
2%	0 hundreds, 0 tens, 2 units	→	0.02

If the percentage is not a whole number, the amount will follow the above rules with the decimal part fitting in appropriately.

For example:

$$17.5\% \rightarrow 0.175$$
$$8.75\% \rightarrow 0.0875$$

Changing a decimal into a percentage

To change a decimal to a percentage it is necessary to multiply by 100%. However, if you consider the template above you can just write out the number.

For example:

$$0.37 \rightarrow 0 \text{ hundreds, 3 tens, 7 units} \rightarrow 37\%$$
$$0.8 \rightarrow 0 \text{ hundreds, 8 tens, 0 units} \rightarrow 80\%$$
$$0.09 \rightarrow 0 \text{ hundreds, 0 tens, 9 units} \rightarrow 9\%$$
$$0.205 \rightarrow 0 \text{ hundreds, 2 ten, 0 units, 5 as decimal} \rightarrow 20.5\%$$

Changing a fraction to a percentage

In order to change a fraction into a percentage you need to ensure that the bottom of the fraction is 100. If this is not initially one hundred, you need to multiply or divide the number at the bottom of the fraction to make 100.
The number multiplied/divided by the bottom also needs to be multiplied/divided by the top number.

The number shown at the top when the bottom is 100 is the percentage.

For example:

$$\frac{9}{25} \times 4 \rightarrow \frac{36}{100} \rightarrow 36\%$$

$$\frac{13}{20} \times 5 \rightarrow \frac{65}{100} \rightarrow 65\%$$

$$\frac{32}{800} \div 8 \rightarrow \frac{4}{100} \rightarrow 4\%$$

Changing a fraction into a decimal

In order to change a fraction to a decimal you need to change the fraction to a percentage as shown above. Once the fraction is a percentage you can then change it to a decimal using the method shown earlier.

However, you could also remember the following:

$$\frac{1}{5} = 0.20 \qquad\qquad \frac{1}{2} = 0.5 \qquad\qquad \frac{1}{10} = 0.1$$

$$\frac{1}{8} = 0.125 \qquad\qquad \frac{1}{4} = 0.25 \qquad\qquad \frac{1}{20} = 0.05$$

If you remember the above, you can multiply by the number you want.

For example:

$$\frac{2}{5} = 0.2 \times 2 \qquad = 0.4$$

$$\frac{3}{8} = 0.125 \times 3 \quad = 0.375$$

$$\frac{4}{10} = 0.1 \times 4 \qquad = 0.4$$

Changing a percentage into a fraction

You need to take away the fraction sign and put the figure over 100. Simplify down if possible.

For example:

$$57\% = \frac{57}{100}$$

$$4\% = \frac{4}{100} = \frac{2}{50} = \frac{1}{25}$$

Changing a decimal into a fraction

You would need to change the decimal into a percentage. The percentage can then be changed into a fraction as shown above.

Now try these:

1. Change the following into fractions in their simplest form:

   a) 43%
   b) 0.71
   c) 0.01
   d) 20%

2. Change the following into decimals:

   a) 5%
   b) $\dfrac{3}{8}$
   c) 23%
   d) $\dfrac{13}{20}$

3. Change the following into percentages:

   a) 0.91
   b) $\dfrac{7}{10}$
   c) 0.03
   d) $\dfrac{3}{5}$

Recurring Decimals

If a decimal is recurring it does not need to be written continuously but instead dots can be used to show the numbers which are repeated. If more than 2 numbers are repeated then a dot will be on top the first number which is repeated, and a dot will be on the last number which is repeated. Any numbers that are in-between the numbers with dots would also be repeated.

For example:

$0.5757575757... = 0.\overset{.}{5}\overset{.}{7}$

$0.432143214321 ... = 0.\overset{.}{4}32\overset{.}{1}$

The part that is repeated can be written as a fraction but depending on how many numbers are repeated depends on what the bottom of the fraction is (the denominator). If 2 numbers are repeated, the denominator would be 99. If 3 numbers are repeated, the denominator would be 999, etc. You would use the one that is required to fit all the numbers in.

For example:

$0.31313131\ldots = 0.\overset{..}{3}\overset{}{1}$

$$= \frac{31}{99}$$

But $0.311311311\ldots = 0.\overset{.}{3}1\overset{.}{1}$

$$= \frac{311}{999}$$

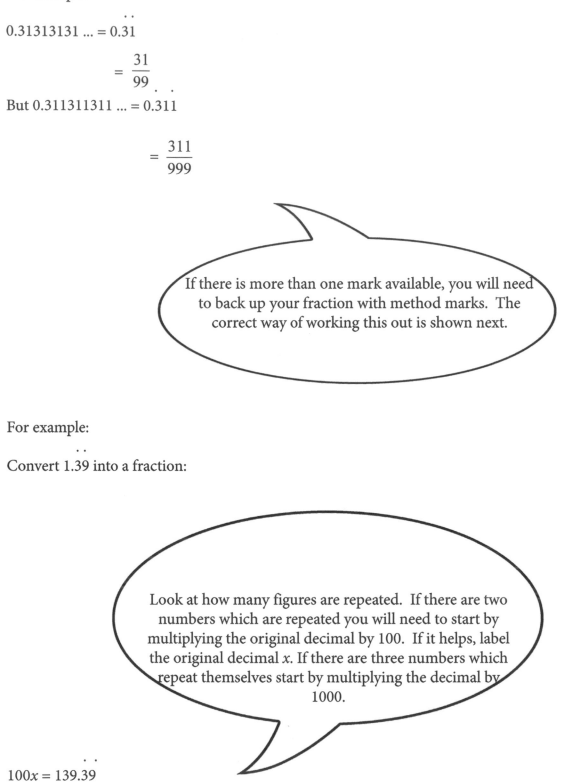

If there is more than one mark available, you will need to back up your fraction with method marks. The correct way of working this out is shown next.

For example:

Convert $1.\overset{..}{3}\overset{}{9}$ into a fraction:

Look at how many figures are repeated. If there are two numbers which are repeated you will need to start by multiplying the original decimal by 100. If it helps, label the original decimal x. If there are three numbers which repeat themselves start by multiplying the decimal by 1000.

$100x = 139.\overset{..}{3}\overset{}{9}$

Once you have multiplied the decimal by 100, deduct the original decimal from the figure you have just found to give you the equivalent of 99 times the decimal amount.

$99x = 139.\overset{..}{3}\overset{}{9} - 1.\overset{..}{3}\overset{}{9}$

This can then be simplified:

$$99x = 138$$

The equation can then be rearranged to get x (the original decimal) on its own:

$$x = \frac{138}{99}$$

$$x = 1\frac{39}{99}$$

Now try these:

1. Convert 5.8̈2 into a fraction.

2. Convert 0.12̇4̇ into a fraction.

Percentage Change

If you are asked to find the percentage change, you need to remember the following formula:

$$\frac{Difference}{Original} \text{ x } 100\%$$

You can remember this as a famous expression of a yellow cartoon character. 'D' stands for difference, 'O' for original and 'H' for multiplying by one hundred.

For example:

If a savings account has £300 in it in February and £240 in April, what is the percentage decrease?

Difference = £60 (£300 - £240)
Original value = £ 300

If you place this into the formula:

$$\frac{60}{300} \times 100\%$$

$$= \frac{6}{30} \times 100\%$$

> Remember, if there is a zero on both the top and bottom of the fraction, you need to remove both as this effectively divides both by ten.

You have already seen that a fraction can be reduced if both the top and bottom of the fraction can be divided by the same number e.g. 2, 3 or 6. In this example divide both the top and bottom of the fraction by 6.

$$= \frac{1}{5} \times 100\%$$

= 20% decrease

Now try these:

1. If there are 40 sweets in a jar on Monday and 24 sweets on Thursday, what is the percentage decrease?

2. If there is £200 in your savings account at the beginning of the month and £350 at the end of month, what is the percentage change?

Compound Interest

Interest, which itself earns interest is known as compound interest.

If a person puts money into a bank account it will earn interest. If no more capital is added to the account the interest will still change, as there will be the original capital and interest in the account each year.

Remember, it is not going to increase by the same amount each year if it is compound interest.

For example:

£1000 is put into an account for 4 years with a guaranteed interest rate of 10%. How much will be in the account at the end of the fourth year?

Year 1: £1000 in the account at start of the year
        10% interest = £100
        Total of £1100 at the end of year 1

Year 2: £1100 in the account at start of the year
        10% interest = £110
        Total of £1210 at the end of year 2

Year 3: £1210 in the account at start of the year
        10% interest = £121
        Total of £1331 at the end of year 3

Year 4: £1331 in the account at start of the year
        10% interest = £133.10
        Total of £1464.10 at the end of year 4

Now try these:

1. A sum of £300 is placed in a bank account on 1 January 2005 which earns interest at 6% per annum compound interest on 31 December each year. How much would be in the account on 1 January 2007?

2. If the value of a house increases by 5% (compounded) each year, how much would a house be worth after 3 years if it was worth £150,000 originally?

3. A sum of £240 is invested at 8% per annum for 4 years. Calculate the total amount in the account including compound interest after the 4 years.

Finding Original Values

Sometimes you may be given a value after it has been reduced and you need to work backwards to find the original value. This could be where a value is reduced in a sale.

Let's have a look at what happens when the amount is a sale price and you want to find out what the price was before the sale.

For example:

You are told that a jacket is £16 in an 80% sale, then 20% of the original price is £16.

20% = £16

To make the 20% become 100%, we can divide it by 20 to find 1% then multiply by 100 to find what the 100% value is.

$$\frac{16}{20} \text{ x } 100 = £80$$

You could also multiply the 16 by 5 to get the 100% value but sometimes the % may not easily changed to 100% so it might be easier to do it the longer way.

Or you can use y as the unknown then rearrange to get it on its own.

As already mentioned, in an 80% sale, 20% of the original price is £16. This can also be written as:

20% of y = £16

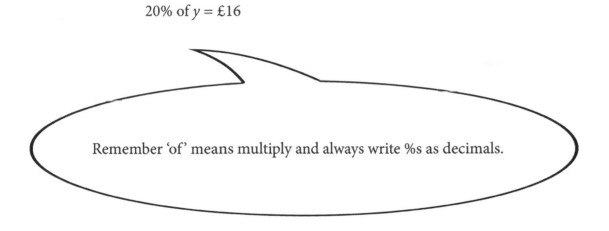

Remember 'of' means multiply and always write %s as decimals.

This translated is 0.20 x y = £16

This can be rearranged to get y on its own:

$$y = \frac{£16}{0.2}$$

y = £80

Now try these:

1. If a wardrobe is £245 in a 30% sale, how much did it cost originally?

2. If a house has increased in price by 20% and is now worth £144,000, how much was it originally worth?

3. If there is a 15% sale and a table is £59.50 in the sale, what was the price before the sale?

Ratios

There will be exam questions where you have to split amounts by a ratio. To help understand the ratio, it is easier to change the ratio into a fraction.

If you add the ratios together, and put the number under each side of the ratio it makes a fraction. Once you have the fraction, you can then find the fraction 'of' the amount.

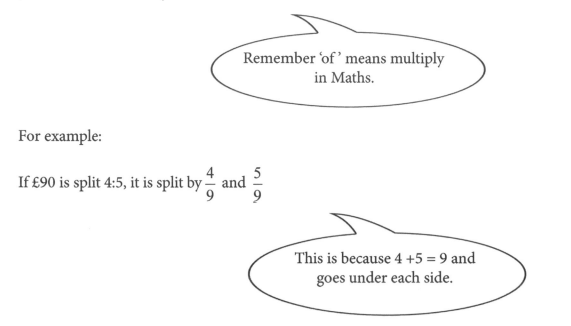

Remember 'of' means multiply in Maths.

For example:

If £90 is split 4:5, it is split by $\dfrac{4}{9}$ and $\dfrac{5}{9}$

This is because 4 + 5 = 9 and goes under each side.

As you have seen in the Percentage section, to find 4 and 5 ninths of £90, you need to divide by 9 and then multiply by 4 and 5.

$$\dfrac{£90}{9} = £10 \times 4 = £40.$$

$$\dfrac{£90}{9} = £10 \times 5 = £50$$

You can then check the split is correct as when numbers are split by a ratio, the newly split amounts should still equal the same total. You should not gain any more or lose any amounts.

This will be exactly the same with larger ratios.

For example:

96 sweets are split with a ratio 1:3:4 between Stephanie, Tom and Harry respectively. How many does each person receive?

Respectively means in the same order.

$1 + 3 + 4 = 8$

$\dfrac{1}{8}$, $\dfrac{3}{8}$ and $\dfrac{4}{8}$

$\dfrac{96}{8} \times 1 = £12$

$\dfrac{96}{8} \times 3 = £36$

$\dfrac{96}{8} \times 4 = £48$

To check: $48 + 36 + 12 = 96$

Now try these:

1. 132 sweets are split with a ratio of 1:2:4:5 between Annie, Tasha, Cerian and Heidi respectively. How many will each person receive?

2. Albert gives Helen, Sean and Kerry £1800 which is split respectively with a ratio of 2:3:4. How much does each person receive?

3. Juliet and Linda split 63 chocolates with a ratio of 3:4 respectively. How many chocolates does each have?

Probability

Probability is another word for chance. The probability of something happening, is also the chance of it happening.

Probability is between 0 and 1 and can be written as a decimal or a fraction.

0 = Impossible
1 = Definitely going to happen

To work out the probability, you need the number of what the question is asking for, divided by the total number of items.

For example:

If there are 19 stamps, 4 are red, 5 are green and 10 are yellow, the probabilities are as shown below:

Probability of green stamp = $\dfrac{5}{19}$

Probability of red stamp = $\dfrac{4}{19}$

Probability of yellow stamp = $\dfrac{10}{19}$

If there are four red stamps, this would be a probability of $\dfrac{4}{19}$.

Typical Questions

Probability is sometimes tested using cards. It is therefore important that you are aware of how many cards are in a deck, the different suits, etc.

For example:

If somebody picks a card, what is the probability of choosing a King?

There are four Kings in a deck of cards out of a total 52 cards. The probability is therefore 4/52 which can be simplified to 1/13 (4 and 52 both divide by 4).

Replacing or not

You could be asked to choose two items. It is possible to pick one, replace it then pick another or pick one, do not replace it and choose another.

For example:

There are five counters in the bag, three are black and two are white. One is chosen, the colour recorded and not replaced. Then a second is chosen, what is the probability of choosing a black counter each time?

First pick = $\dfrac{3}{5}$

Second pick = $\dfrac{2}{4}$

(This is because there are now only 2 black counters and a total of four in the bag).

The 'And' and 'Or' rule

'And' = 'x'
'Or' = '+'

For example:

What is the probability of picking a King or a Queen from a deck of cards?

Probability of King 'or' Probability of Queen

$$\frac{4}{52} + \frac{4}{52} = \frac{8}{52} = \frac{2}{13}$$

Where the bottom of the fractions are the same, you can add the tops together.

For example:

What is the probability of picking a King and a Queen from a deck of cards if the first card is picked, replaced and a second card is chosen?

Probability of King 'and' Probability of Queen

$$\frac{4}{52} \quad \text{x} \quad \frac{4}{52} \quad = \frac{16}{2704} = \frac{1}{169} \text{ (divide top and bottom by 16)}$$

Tree Diagrams

To assist you when answering probability questions, you need to remember the following template:

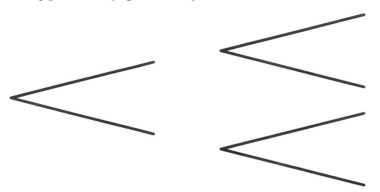

Each point is your option, at each of these points you face a decision. Each branch adds up to 1 because you either do something or you don't.

You may be given a question where you don't know the background. You will then need to complete the tree diagram with missing probabilities. All you will need to remember is that the 'branches' all add up to one.

For example:

Complete the tree diagram

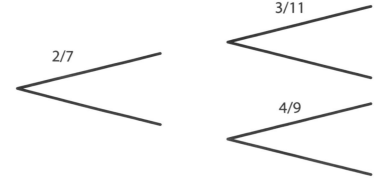

As you will see below, the red probabilities are the answers. You do not need to know any background about the question, it is not necessary if we know one of the probabilities on the 'branch'.

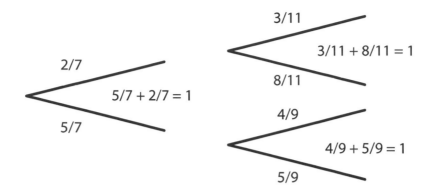

However, you will most likely be given a question where you need to work out all of the probabilities on the 'branches'.

For example:

Ten sweets are in a bag, 7 are lemon and 3 are cola. Find the probabilities of different outcomes when one sweet is chosen, not replaced and then another is chosen.

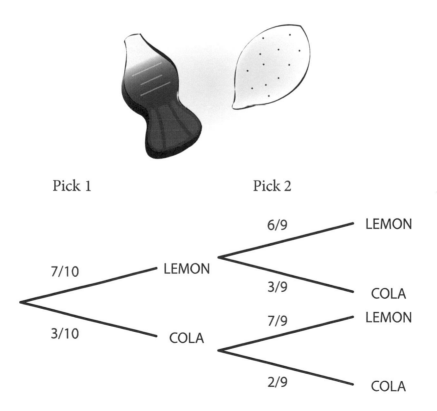

Pick 1   Pick 2

<u>Pick 1</u>
You could either choose a lemon sweet or a cola sweet. There are 7 lemon sweets out of a possible 10 sweets so the probability of picking a lemon sweet is 7/10.

There are 3 cola sweets in the bag so you could pick one of the 3 cola sweets from a possible 10, giving the probability as 3/10.

<u>Pick 2</u>

The probabilities will depend on the outcome of the first pick.

If you chose a lemon sweet in the first pick, there will be only 6 lemon sweets left in the bag out of the total 9 sweets. This is because you did not replace the sweet that was chosen first so there is one less sweet in the bag. Therefore the probability of choosing another lemon sweet will be 6/9.

The probability of picking a cola sweet in the second pick, if you chose the lemon sweet in the first pick, would be 3/9. This is because there will still be all 3 colas left out of a possible 9 sweets.

If you chose a cola sweet in the first pick, there are still 7 lemon sweets left in the bag out of the total 9 sweets. Therefore the probability of choosing a lemon sweet will be 7/9.

The probability of picking another cola sweet in the second pick, if you chose the cola sweet in the first pick, would be 2/9. This is because there will now be only 2 cola sweets left out of a possible 9 sweets.

The probabilities will look like this:

Lemon 'and' Lemon

$$\frac{7}{10} \times \frac{6}{9} = \frac{42}{90} = \frac{7}{15} \text{ (divide both top and bottom by 6)}$$

Lemon 'and' Cola

$$\frac{7}{10} \times \frac{3}{9} = \frac{21}{90} = \frac{7}{30} \text{ (divide both top and bottom by 3)}$$

Cola 'and' Lemon

$$\frac{3}{10} \times \frac{7}{9} = \frac{21}{90} = \frac{7}{30} \text{ (divide both top and bottom by 3)}$$

Cola 'and' Cola

$$\frac{3}{10} \times \frac{2}{9} = \frac{6}{90} = \frac{1}{15} \text{ (divide both top and bottom by 6)}$$

You will see that all the outcomes add up to one as you will definitely choose one of the paths, there are no other possible answers.

If asked for the probability of two sweets which are the same flavour it will either be two cola sweets or two lemon sweets.

... So   P(Cola) 'and' P(Cola)   'or'   P(Lemon) 'and' P(Lemon)

$$= \frac{1}{15} + \frac{7}{15}$$

$$= \frac{8}{15}$$

42

Now try these:

1. Twelve sweets are in a bag, 8 are strawberry and 4 are apple. Find the probabilities of different outcomes when one sweet is chosen, replaced and then another is chosen.

2. If two cards are chosen out of a deck of cards, what is the probability of a choosing two aces if one card is chosen, not replaced then a second card is picked?

3. If the probability of it raining in the Summer is 0.32, what is the probability of it not raining?

Section 3 – Areas and Volumes

Areas and Volumes of Shapes

Volume = length x length x length

Area = length x length

Triangle

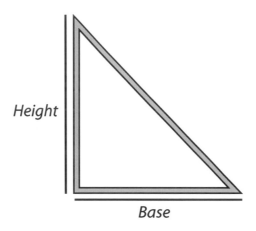

Area= ½ x base x height

Rectangle

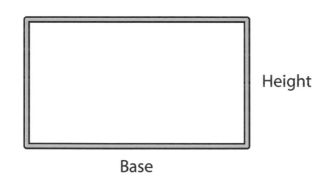

Area = base x height

Cuboid

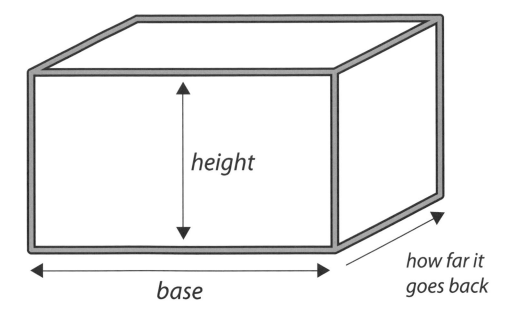

Surface area = base x height (rectangle)
Volume = surface area x how far it goes back.

Prism

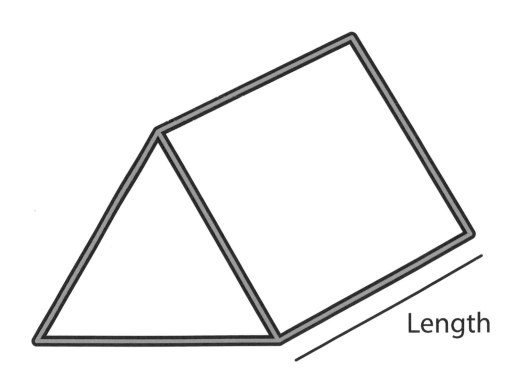

Volume = area of cross section x length.

Sphere

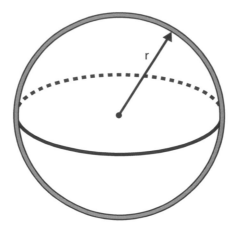

Volume $= \dfrac{4}{3}\pi r^3$

Surface area $= 4\pi r^2$

Cone

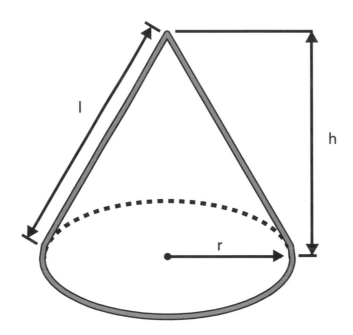

Volume $= \dfrac{1}{3}\pi r^2 h$

Curved surface area $= \pi r l$

Trapezium

Trapeziums are easy to recognise as they have two parallel lines. Think of these as train tracks. They must be parallel otherwise the trains could crash at some point.

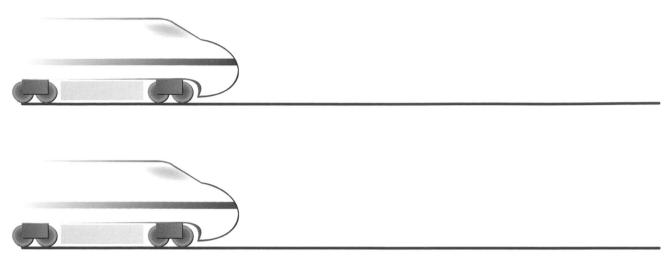

A trapezium is a mixture of rectangles and triangles. It could have a triangle on both ends of the rectangle or only one. It could be vertical or horizontal.

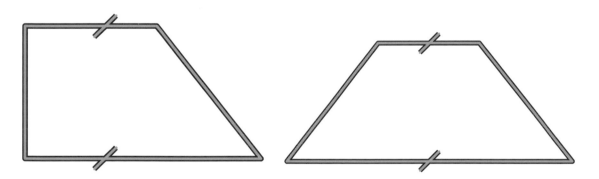

The formula for the area of a trapezium is:

$$\frac{1}{2}\,(a + b) \text{ x height.}$$

This is where *a* and *b* are the two parallel sides.

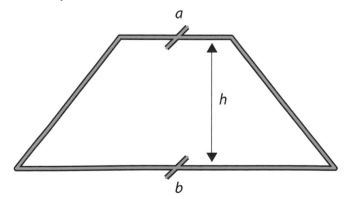

The exam paper may extend the trapezium by adding volume to the question.

Volume = surface area x how far it goes back

For example:

Find the volume of shape *A*

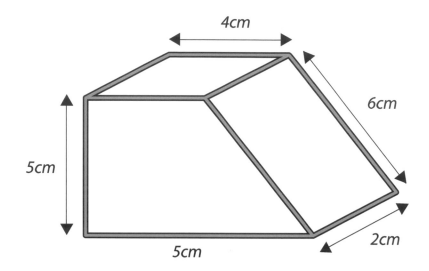

Volume = $\frac{1}{2}$ (*a* + *b*) x height x how far it goes back

Area = $\frac{1}{2}$ (5 + 4) x 5

$\quad = \frac{1}{2}$ x 9 x 5

$\quad = \frac{1}{2}$ x 45

$\quad = 22.5$ cm²

Volume = 22.5 x 2
$\qquad = 45$ cm³

Cylinders

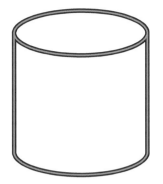

Volume = area of circle x how far it goes back

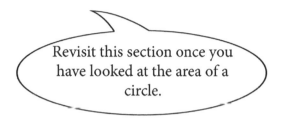

Revisit this section once you have looked at the area of a circle.

For example:

Find the volume of the cylinder.

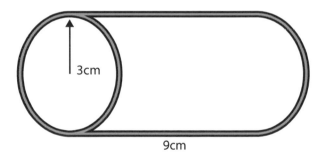

3cm

9cm

Volume = πr² x 9
       = π x 3² x 9
       = π x 9 x 9
       = 81π cm³
       = 254.47 cm³ (2dp)

Now try these:

1. Find the area of:

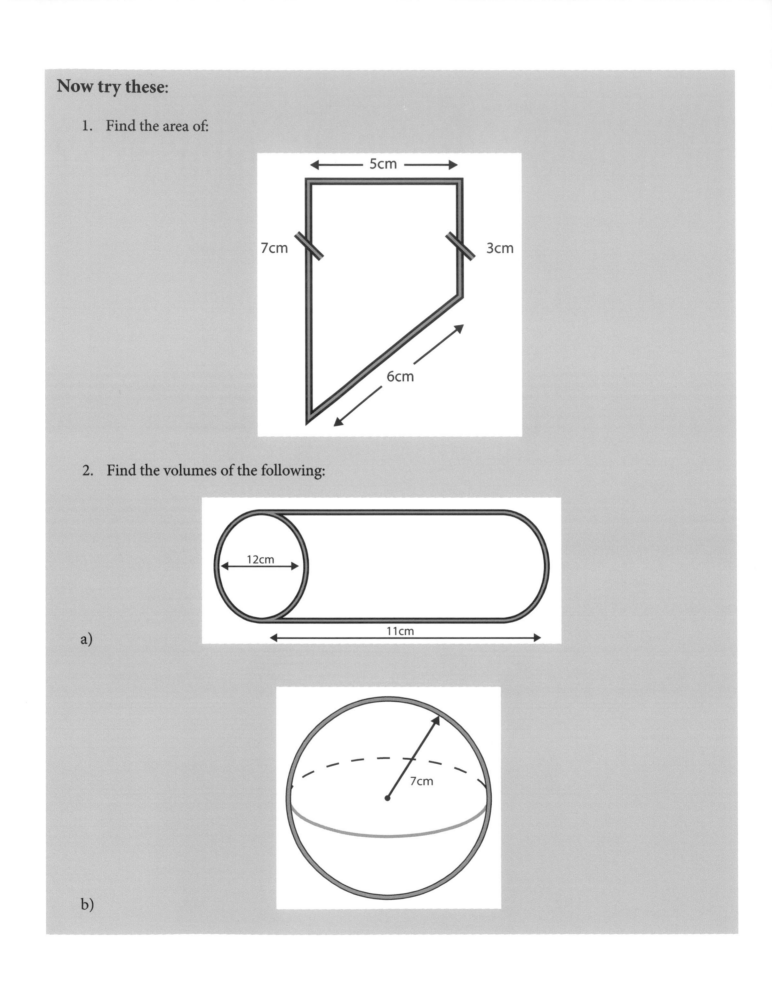

2. Find the volumes of the following:

a)

b)

Areas and Volumes with algebra

Examiners may use algebra within area/volume questions. Rather than calculating the area/volumes of shapes as a number, you may need to recognise an area/volume as an algebraic expression.

Remember that an area is a length multiplied by a length, and a volume is a length multiplied by a length, multiplied by another length. You will then be fine. The lengths may be given to you as an unknown and you may then need to work out how many lengths are being multiplied.

You may also be told that some values have no dimensions, this could be integers and even π. If you are told these values have no dimensions then they are not counted as lengths and are effectively ignored.

For example, if x, y and z are all lengths, the following could be areas:

$$\frac{x^2 y}{z\pi} \qquad \frac{xz^2 y}{4xz} \qquad \frac{3xz^3}{y^2}$$

All of the above are effectively a length multiplied by a length. If there are more than two lengths multiplied together, there is at least one dividing to cancel it out.

There may also be some numbers used which do not have any dimensions. This means that the numbers do not count as a length.

Think of the area of a circle (πr^2). The radius is a length but π represents a number. The circle area is therefore made up of a length multiplied by a length. This is the same for the area of a triangle ($\frac{1}{2}bh$) as the base and height are both lengths but the $\frac{1}{2}$ is not a length.

For example:

If x, y, z are lengths, and π, 2, 3, 4 have no dimensions, label the following areas/ volumes.

	$\dfrac{3y^2 x}{z\pi}$	$\dfrac{2z^3 yx}{4x^2}$	$3xyz$	$\dfrac{3y^2 x}{z\pi}$	$2\pi x^2$
Area/Volume?					

Ignore the numbers with no dimensions:

	$\dfrac{y^2 x}{z}$	$\dfrac{z^3 yx}{x^2}$	xyz	$\dfrac{y^2 x}{z}$	x^2
Area/Volume?					

If you change these all into lengths you have:

	$\dfrac{l^3}{l}$	$\dfrac{l^5}{l^2}$	l^3	$\dfrac{l^3}{l}$	l^2
Area/Volume?	l^2 = Area	l^3 = Volume	Volume	l^2 = Area	Area

You may be given an equation with two parts, for example:

$xy + z^2$
$xy^2 + z$
$3x\pi + 2y^3$

Where this is the case, think logically…
A volume plus a volume make a bigger volume.
A length plus a length make a longer length.

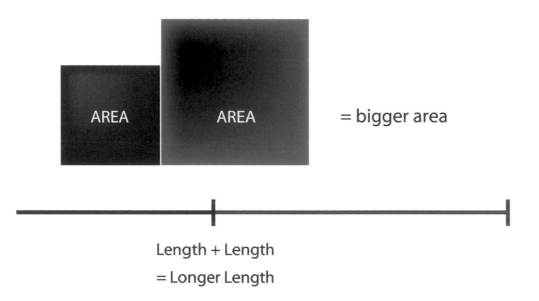

However, if you have a mixture of the two they will stay as they are. A length plus an area is just a length plus an area. It would not become an area, it would not become a length. You need to take care when answering these type of questions.

Now try these:

1.

If r, s, t are lengths, and π, 2, 3, 4 have no dimensions, label the following areas/ volumes.

	$\dfrac{4rst}{3\pi}$	$\dfrac{4t^2s}{3r} + \dfrac{3s^3}{2r}$	$2\pi r^2$	$\dfrac{3r^2s^3t}{st^2}$	$4rt^2 + \dfrac{3s^2r}{2}$
Area/Volume?					

2.

If m, n, p are lengths, and π, 5, 6, 7 have no dimensions, what are the following?

$7mp + 7n^2$	$\dfrac{pn^2}{7m} + \dfrac{6p^3}{m^2\pi}$	$5\pi pmn$	$\dfrac{6pm^2}{n\pi} + \dfrac{n^2p}{m^2}$
?	?	?	?

Circles

You may be asked to find one of the following:

- Area of circle
- Circumference of circle
- Radius of circle
- Diameter of circle

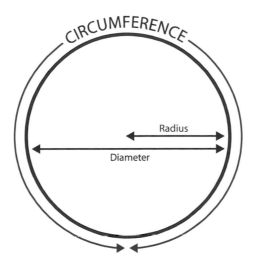

Area of circle = $\pi \times r^2$ (πr^2)

You can remember this as 'pies are squared' as it is now possible to buy square shaped pies. Remember you tell someone that pies are squared, you don't ask so it is not the other way around.

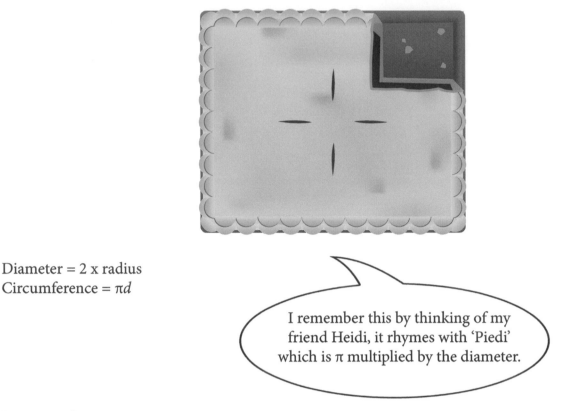

Diameter = 2 x radius
Circumference = πd

I remember this by thinking of my friend Heidi, it rhymes with 'Piedi' which is π multiplied by the diameter.

For example:

If the area of circle is 25π, what would the diameter be?

$\pi \times r^2 = 25\pi$
$r^2 = 25$
$r = 5cm$ $\quad\quad d = 2 \times 5 = 10cm$

If the circumference of a circle is 12π, what is the area?

$\pi d = 12\pi$
$d = 12$ $\quad\quad r = 6cm$

Area $= \pi r^2$
$\quad\quad = \pi \times 36$
$\quad\quad = 113cm^2$ (3sf)

You may also be asked questions which will test your knowledge of other shapes.

For example:

Find the area of shaded part

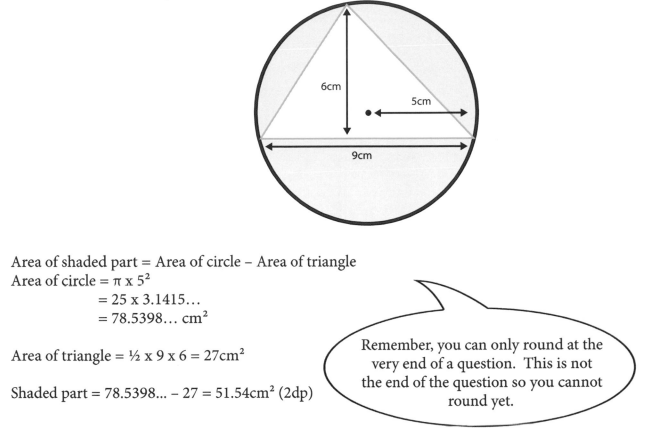

Area of shaded part = Area of circle – Area of triangle
Area of circle = π x 5²
$\qquad$ = 25 x 3.1415…
$\qquad$ = 78.5398… cm²

Area of triangle = ½ x 9 x 6 = 27cm²

Shaded part = 78.5398… – 27 = 51.54cm² (2dp)

Remember, you can only round at the very end of a question. This is not the end of the question so you cannot round yet.

Now try these:

1. What is the area of a circle if the diameter is 7cm?

2. What is the circumference of a circle if the radius is 5cm?

3. Find the area of shaded part to 3dp.

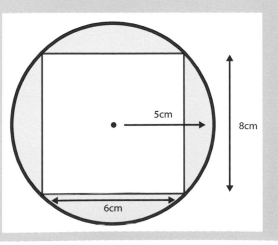

Sectors & Segments

Sectors

A sector is part of a circle so once you are happy with circles, you should be also able to answer these questions.

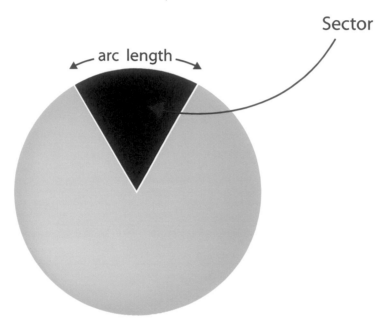

All you need to remember is that a circle is made up of 360° and if you are given a sector of a circle it will be part of the 360°.

You have already seen the area and circumference of a circle which is for the full 360°, so the formulas will change slightly for the sector. Part of the circumference which is for the sector is called an arc.

$$\text{Sector area} = \pi \times r^2 \times \frac{n}{360}$$

$$\text{Arc length} = \pi \times d \times \frac{n}{360}$$

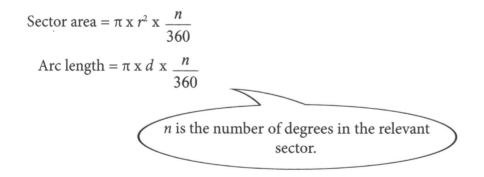

n is the number of degrees in the relevant sector.

For example:

Find the area of the sector and the arc length

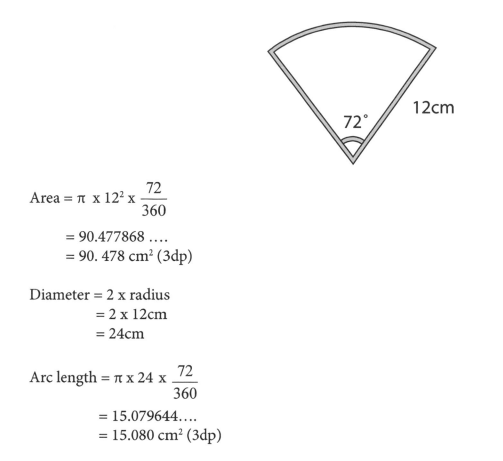

Area $= \pi \times 12^2 \times \dfrac{72}{360}$

      $= 90.477868 \ldots$
      $= 90.478 \text{ cm}^2 \text{ (3dp)}$

Diameter $= 2 \times$ radius
        $= 2 \times 12\text{cm}$
        $= 24\text{cm}$

Arc length $= \pi \times 24 \times \dfrac{72}{360}$

      $= 15.079644 \ldots$
      $= 15.080 \text{ cm}^2 \text{ (3dp)}$

Take care if you are asked to find the perimeter of the sector. This would be all the way around the sector so the radius would need to be added twice to the arc length.

For example:

Find the perimeter of sector A to 2dp

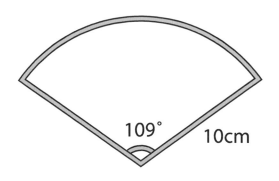

Diameter $= 2 \times$ radius
        $= 2 \times 10\text{cm}$
        $= 20\text{cm}$

Circumference $= \pi \times 20 \times \dfrac{109}{360}$

$\qquad = 19.024088\ldots$ cm

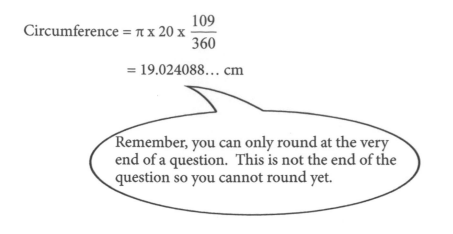

Remember, you can only round at the very end of a question. This is not the end of the question so you cannot round yet.

Perimeter = Arc length + radius + radius
$\qquad = 19.024088\ldots$ cm + 10cm + 10cm
$\qquad = 39.024088\ldots$ cm
$\qquad = 39.02$ cm (2dp)

Segments

A segment is part of a sector of a circle, which is split into two by a line. It goes from one side of the circle to the other, this is called a chord.

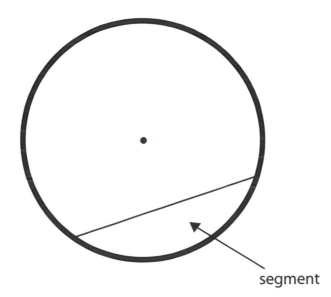

segment

In order to find the area of a segment find the area of the sector then take away the triangle using the formula for the area of a triangle which you will see under the 'Sine and Cosine rule' section.

For example:

Find the shaded area:

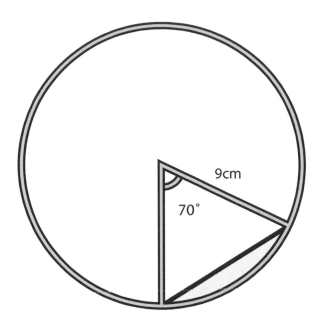

The area of a 70° sector is calculated as follows:

$$\pi \times 9^2 \times \frac{70°}{360°} = 49.48008429..... \ cm^2$$

The area of the triangle is calculated as follows:

$$\frac{1}{2} \times 9cm \times 9cm \times Sin\ 70° = 38.05755114.... \ cm^2$$

Remember, even though you may only be given one length of the sector, the lengths are the radius so they are the same amount.

The area of the segment will therefore be the difference between the sector and the triangle:

$$49.48008429... - 38.05755114... = 11.422533.... \ cm^2$$
$$= 11.4 \ cm^2 \ (3sf)$$

Remember, you cannot round until the end of a question.

Now try these:

1. Find the area of the sector to 2dp

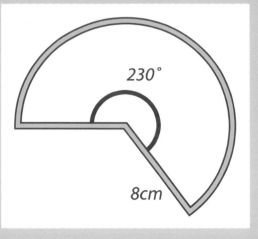

2. Find the arc length of the sector to 3sf

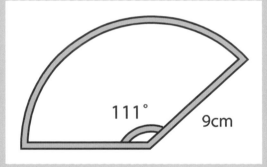

3. Find the perimeter of the sector

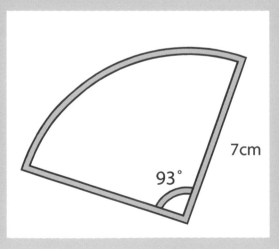

4. Find the area of the shaded section shown below:

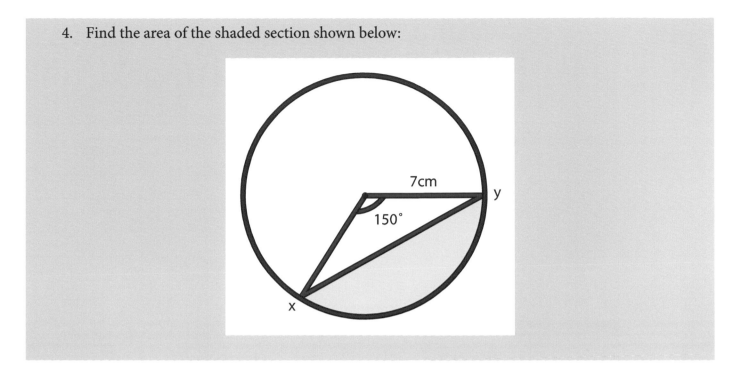

Section 4 – Triangles

Types of Triangles

There are four main triangles which are tested in GCSE Maths. These are shown below.

Isosceles

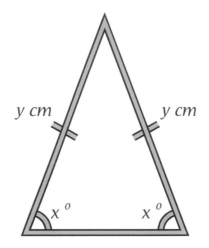

- Two sides have the same length.
- Two angles have the same size.
- If given one angle, you can find the others.

Equilateral Triangle

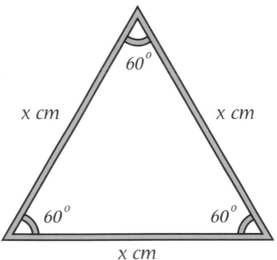

- All angles are the same (60°)
- All lengths are the same

Right Angled Triangle

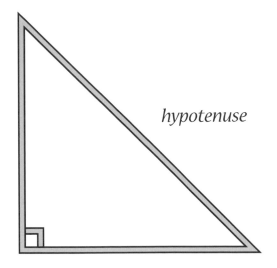

- If you see a right angled triangle, you need to consider Pythagorus Theorem and Trigonometry.
- The longest side of the right angled triangle is the diagonal (hypotenuse).

Scalene

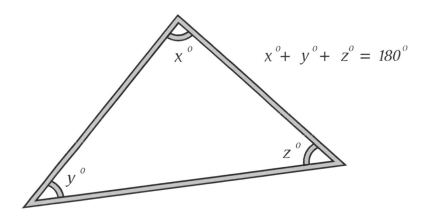

$x^o + y^o + z^o = 180^o$

- None of the previously mentioned triangles.
- No angles or sides of the triangle are the same.

Things to remember:

There are 180° in a triangle.
Angles on a straight line total 180°.

For example:

Find x

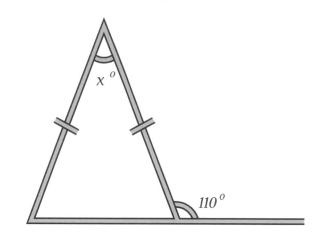

Angles on a straight line = 180°
180° - 110° = 70°

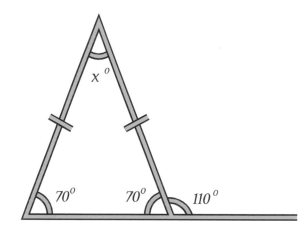

Angles in a triangle add up to 180°
70° + 70° + x = 180°
140° + x = 180°
x = 180° - 140°
x = 40°

Now try these:

1. Find *t*

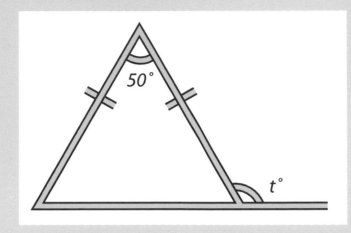

2. Find *x* if the perimeter is 21cm.

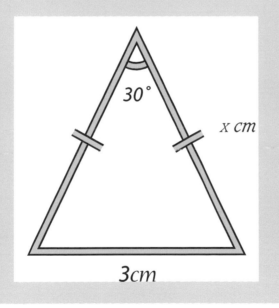

Pythagorus Theorem

- Used on a right angled triangle
- You will have all three lengths of the triangle at the end
- You are given two lengths, but have to find the third
- You either have the hypotenuse (the longest side) or you are finding it

The formula: $a^2 + b^2 = c^2$

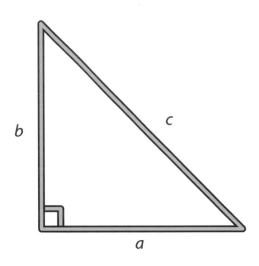

This can be remembered as:

$$\text{Missing length} = \sqrt{\text{Longest side}^2 \pm \text{Smallest side}^2}$$

The '± sign' means you can either add or minus at this point.

- If you have the hypotenuse the sign is a minus.
- If you are finding the hypotenuse, add the two squared amounts together.

An easy way to remember this is to look at how many values of sides touch the right angle. One side is a minus, and two sides is a plus because a minus and a minus make a plus.

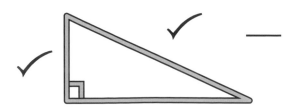

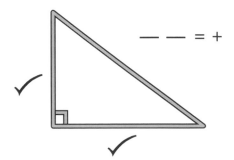

Typical Questions

It is very unlikely that you will be given a straight forward question asking you to find the missing length. It is more likely you will be asked to find either the perimeter or the area of the triangle.

Perimeter

If you are asked to find the perimeter of a triangle, two sides will be given and you will need to find the third. Once you have all the sides you can add all three together to get the perimeter.

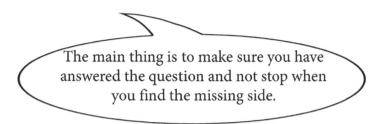

The main thing is to make sure you have answered the question and not stop when you find the missing side.

Area

To find the area of a triangle you need to be able to complete the following formula:

0.5 x base x height

It is likely that the two sides given will not be the base and the height. You will therefore need to use Pythagorus Theorem to find the missing side and complete the formula.

For example:

1) Find the area of triangle

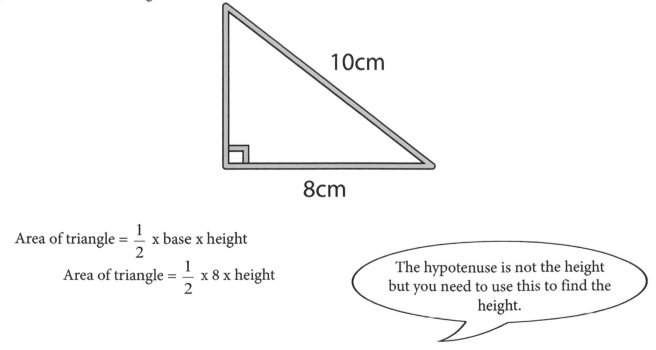

10cm

8cm

Area of triangle = $\frac{1}{2}$ x base x height

Area of triangle = $\frac{1}{2}$ x 8 x height

The hypotenuse is not the height but you need to use this to find the height.

67

Height $= \sqrt{10^2 - 8^2}$

$= \sqrt{100 - 64}$

$= \sqrt{36}$

$= 6\text{ cm}$

Area: $\dfrac{1}{2}$ x 8 x 6

$= \dfrac{1}{2}$ x 48

$= 24\text{ cm}^2$

2) Find perimeter of triangle

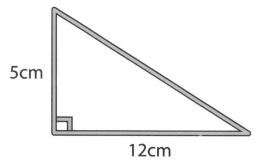

Perimeter = All sides added together

12cm + 5cm + ??

Third side $= \sqrt{12^2 + 5^2}$

$= \sqrt{144 + 25}$

$= \sqrt{169}$

$= 13\text{ cm}$

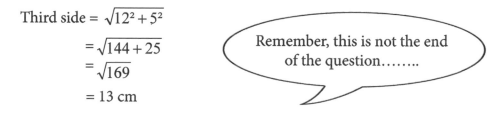

Remember, this is not the end of the question........

Perimeter = 12cm + 5cm + 13cm = 30cm

Now try these:

1. Find *h*

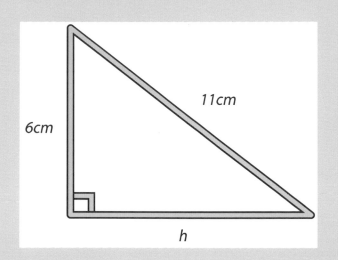

2. Find perimeter of triangle to 2*dp*

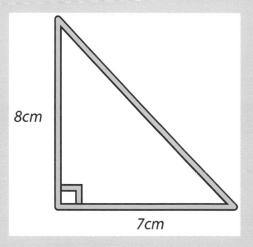

3. Find area of triangle

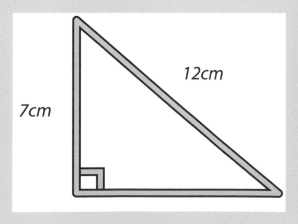

Trigonometry

- Will be using a right angled triangle
- You will have two lengths and one angle at the end

You are either:
- Given one length and one angle, find another length or……
- Given two lengths, find an angle

There is always a side that you don't know and you don't want to know. By recognising this side you will be able to choose the correct formula.

Step 1:
Label the triangle.

Each triangle will have a hypotenuse (the diagonal), the opposite of the angle in the triangle and the adjacent which touches both the angle and the right angle.

Some examples are shown below:

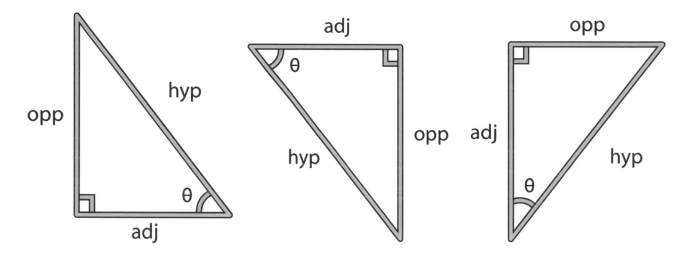

Step 2
Next decide which side you don't have and do not want to know. Choose the formula below that does not contain that side.

$$\text{Sin } \theta = \frac{opp}{hyp} \qquad\qquad \text{Cos } \theta = \frac{adj}{hyp} \qquad\qquad \text{Tan } \theta = \frac{opp}{adj}$$

You need to learn the above formulas as these are not given on the formula sheet. These could be remembered using the anagram below:

'Silly Old Hector Can't Add Hundreds Tens Or Anything'

I	P	Y		O	D	Y		A	P	D
N	P	P		S	J	P		N	P	J

Each trigonometry function (sin, cos and tan) is followed by θ and is then equal to the next two sides in a fraction. E.g. $\sin \theta = \dfrac{opp}{hyp}$

Step 3

The equation needs to be completed using the values shown although there will be one unknown. This equation should then be rearranged to get the unknown on its own.

This will be slightly different if you are finding θ.

For example:

$$\text{Tan } \theta = \frac{8}{10}$$

The algebra section confirms that you need to move things away from the unknown. In this case move 'tan' away from the unknown which is θ. The opposite of 'tan' is 'tan⁻¹', this then moves to the other side and 'joins the back of the queue'.

$$\theta = \frac{8}{10} \tan^{-1}$$

'Tan⁻¹' is achieved by pressing the 'shift' or '2nd function' key on the calculator before the 'tan' button.

You can remember this by typing the equation into the calculator backwards and using 'shift' for θ.

For example:

$$\text{Tan } \theta = \frac{8}{10}$$

[8] [÷] [10] [=] [shift] [tan]

There are some calculators which may require you to input the calculation the other way but these are very rare. If your calculator does not work using the method above you will need to input the figures as follows:

For example:

1) Find area of triangle

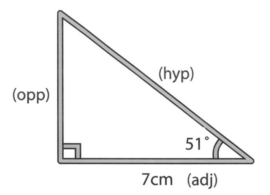

(hyp)

(opp)

51°

7cm   (adj)

Area of triangle = ½ x base x height
Area of triangle = ½ x 7 x ?

$Tan\ \theta = \dfrac{opp}{adj}$

$Tan\ 51 = \dfrac{opp}{7}$

7 x tan 51 = opp

Using the calculator you see that: opp = 8.644280096…..

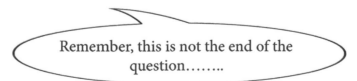

Remember, this is not the end of the question……..

Area of triangle = ½ x 7 x 8.64428096

Area of triangle = 30.25498034
             = 30.25 cm²

Remember, you only round at the end of the question.

2) Find θ

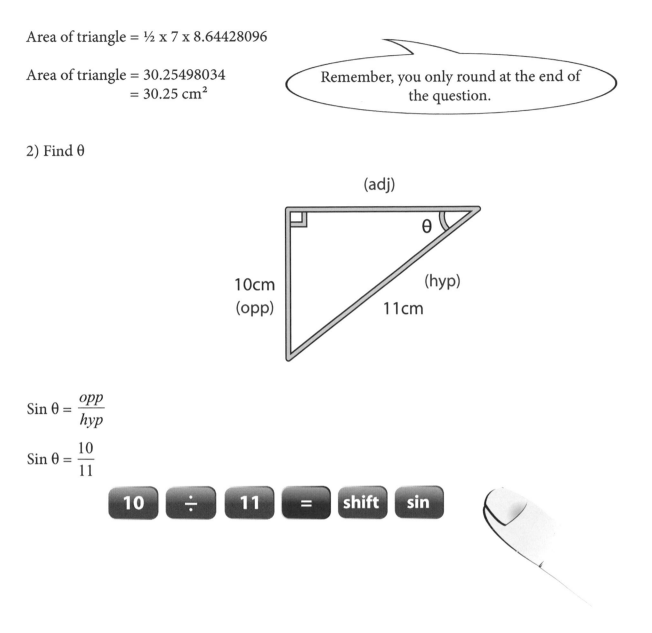

Sin θ = $\dfrac{opp}{hyp}$

Sin θ = $\dfrac{10}{11}$

θ = 65.38002267

θ = 65.38° (2dp)

Now try these:

1. Find θ

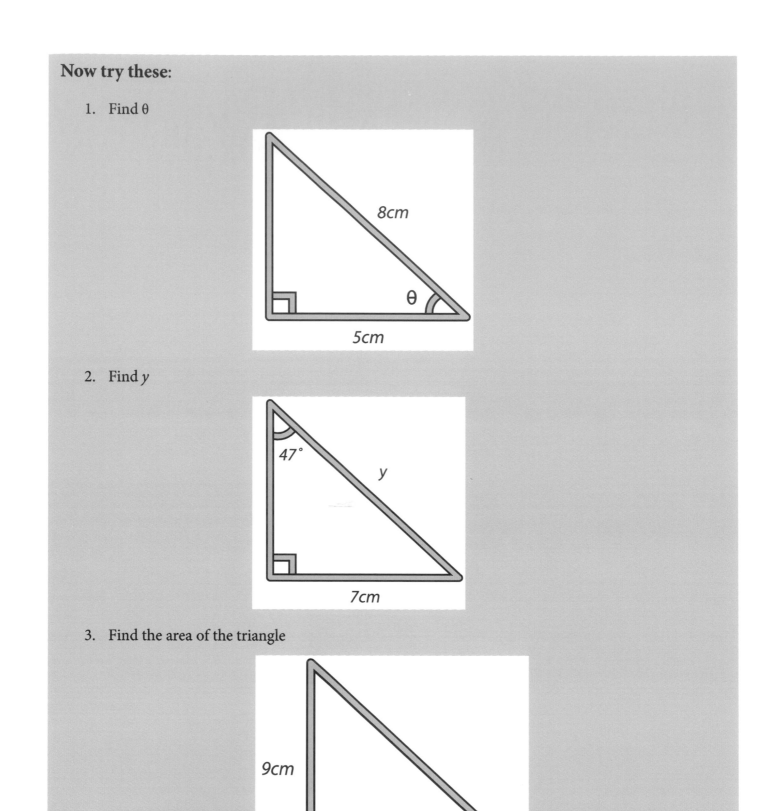

2. Find *y*

3. Find the area of the triangle

Similar Triangles

If triangles are described as 'similar' it means that one is an enlargement of the other.

For example:

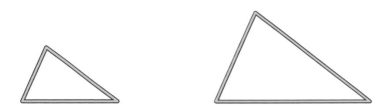

There will always be the same two sides that are provided on the two triangles so you will be able to work out the scale factor. The scale factor is the multiple that one triangle is multiplied by, to create the second triangle.

This can be found by dividing the largest of these sides by the other. This will give the scale factor.

For example:

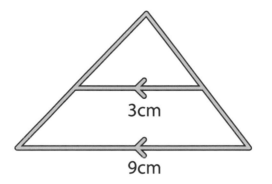

3cm

9cm

You need to think how 3 would become 9.

This would be multiplied by 3 so this would be the scale factor. Once you have worked out the scale factor, you are then able to find any missing values.

For example:

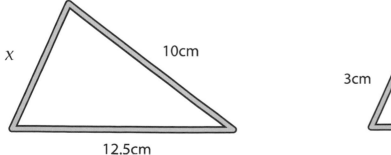

x

10cm

12.5cm

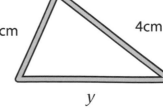

3cm

4cm

y

Looking at the diagrams you can see that 4 becomes 10 by being multiplied by 2.5. This is therefore the scale factor.

$x = 3 \times 2.5$
$x = 7.5$ cm

$y = 12.5 \div 2.5$
$y = 5$ cm

Now try these:

1. If the triangles below are similar, find r and t.

2. Find f and g

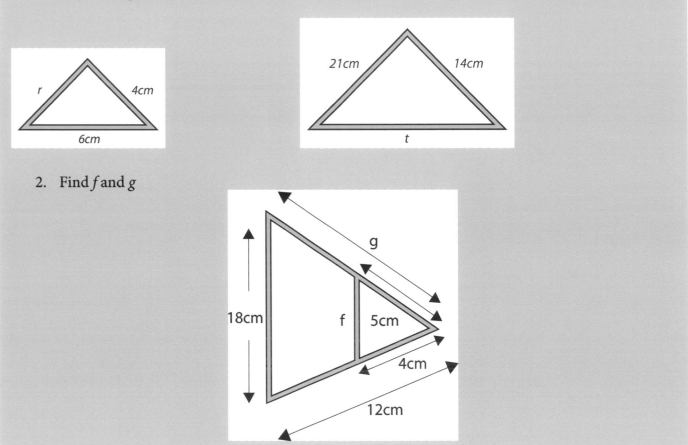

Sine & Cosine Rule

You have previously used trigonometry to find missing lengths and angles in triangles but only in right angled triangles.

When the triangle does not have a right angle, you need to use either the sine rule or the cosine rule. The formulas below are included on the formula sheet so you do not need to learn them.

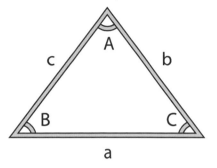

Sine Rule

$$\frac{a}{SinA} = \frac{b}{SinB} = \frac{c}{SinC}$$

The sine rule is to be used when you have a complete 'pair'. By 'pair' it means that you have an angle and the opposite side. At the end of the question, after using the sine rule, you should have two complete 'pairs'.

Although the formula is shown with the missing angles on the bottom of the fraction, this can be swapped around so that the angles are on the top as shown below:

$$\frac{SinA}{a} = \frac{SinB}{b} = \frac{SinC}{c}$$

This is what you need to do if you are finding the missing angle.

For example:

Find x

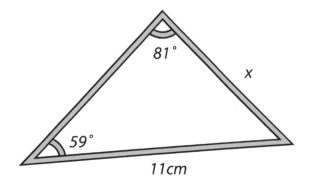

$$\frac{x}{Sin59} = \frac{11}{Sin81}$$

$$x = \frac{11}{Sin81} \times Sin\ 59$$

$x = 9.55$ (2dp)

For example:

Find y

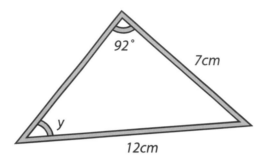

$$\frac{Siny}{7} = \frac{Sin92}{12}$$

$$Sin\ y = \frac{Sin92}{12} \times 7$$

$Sin\ y = 0.5829\ldots\ldots$
$\quad y = 35.66$ (2dp)

Cosine Rule

$a^2 = b^2 + c^2 - 2bcCosA$

The cosine rule is used for a non right angled triangles where you are finding either a length or an angle, but do not have a 'pair' already. However, by finding the unknown this should complete a 'pair'.

The cosine rule will either find an angle or a length. The key thing to remember is that the unknown will be 'a' if it is the missing length or 'A' if you are finding the missing angle.

You will of course be given the formula below:

$$a^2 = b^2 + c^2 - 2bcCos\ A$$

If you are finding a missing angle, the equation needs to be rearranged as:

$$\text{Cos } A = \frac{b^2 + c^2 - a^2}{2bc}$$

This is because:

$$a^2 = b^2 + c^2 - 2bc\text{Cos } A$$
$$a^2 - b^2 - c^2 = -2bc\text{Cos } A$$
$$\frac{a^2 - b^2 - c^2}{-2bc} = \text{Cos } A$$
$$\frac{b^2 + c^2 - a^2}{2bc} = \text{Cos } A$$

For example:

Find Θ

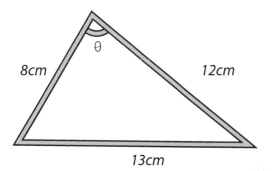

$$\text{Cos } A = \frac{b^2 + c^2 - a^2}{2bc}$$

$$\text{Cos } \Theta = \frac{12^2 + 8^2 - 13^2}{2(12)(8)}$$

$$\text{Cos } \Theta = \frac{144 + 64 - 169}{192}$$

$$\text{Cos } \Theta = \frac{39}{192}$$

$$\Theta = 78.28 \text{ (2dp)}$$

For example:

Find x

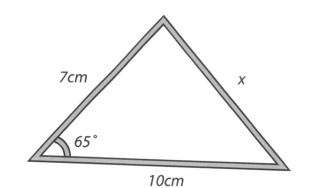

$a^2 = b^2 + c^2 - 2bc\text{Cos } A$

$x^2 = 7^2 + 10^2 - 2(7)(10)\text{Cos } 65$

$x^2 = 49 + 100 - 140\text{Cos } 65$

$x^2 = 149 - 140\text{Cos } 65$

$x^2 = 149 - 140(0.4226182....)$

$x^2 = 149 - 59.166556...$

$x^2 = 89.83344....$

$x = \sqrt{89.8334433...}$

$x = 9.478 \text{ (3dp)}$

You need to ask yourself the following questions:

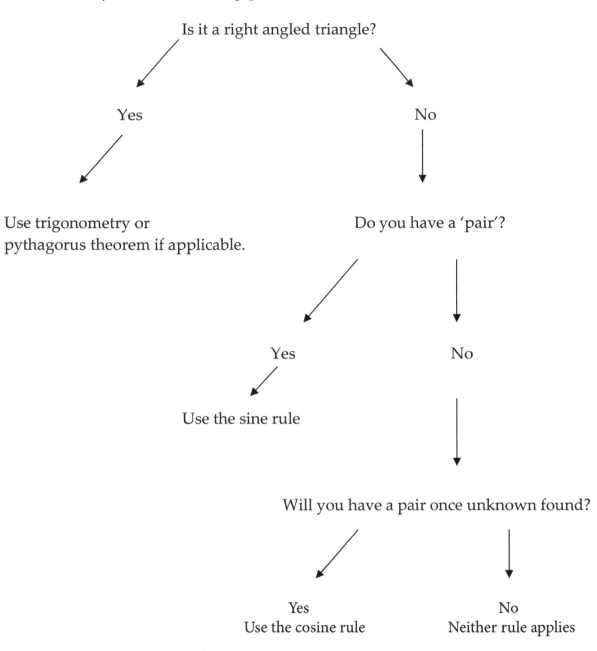

Is it a right angled triangle?

Yes

No

Use trigonometry or pythagorus theorem if applicable.

Do you have a 'pair'?

Yes

No

Use the sine rule

Will you have a pair once unknown found?

Yes
Use the cosine rule

No
Neither rule applies

Area of triangle

You may be asked to find the area of a triangle where there are triangles just like the ones given for the sine and cosine rule. If you have an angle in the triangle this is a big hint that you need to use the formula.

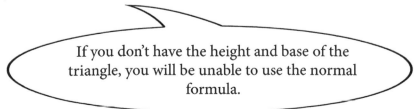

If you don't have the height and base of the triangle, you will be unable to use the normal formula.

The formula you need to use for finding this is:

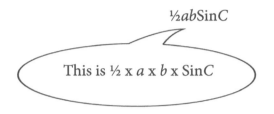

½*ab*SinC

This is ½ x *a* x *b* x SinC

When using the same triangle as the cosine and sine rule, you need to label up the triangle. Use an angle and two sides but not the side that is opposite the angle that you use.

For example:

Find the area of the triangle below:

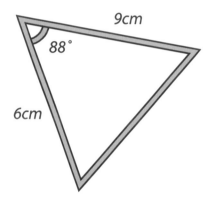

9cm

88°

6cm

The angle will represent '*C*' and the other lengths will become '*a*' and '*b*'. These values can then go into the formula ½*ab*SinC.

½ x 6 x 9 x Sin88°
= 26.98 cm² (2dp)

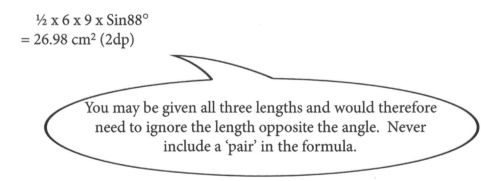

You may be given all three lengths and would therefore need to ignore the length opposite the angle. Never include a 'pair' in the formula.

Now try these:

1. Find ϴ

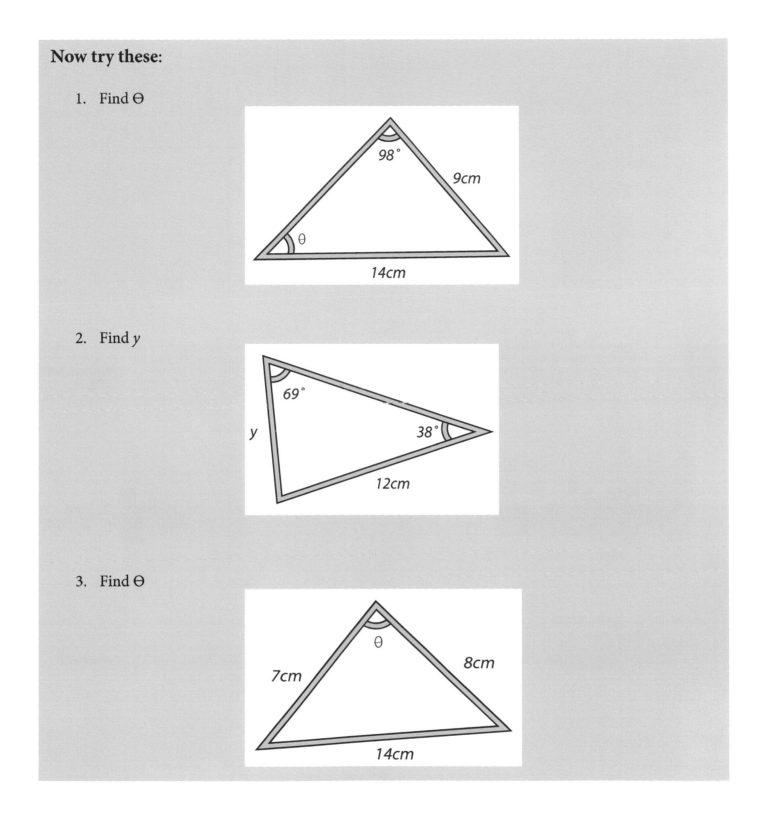

98°

9cm

θ

14cm

2. Find *y*

69°

y

38°

12cm

3. Find ϴ

θ

7cm

8cm

14cm

4. Find the area of the triangle:

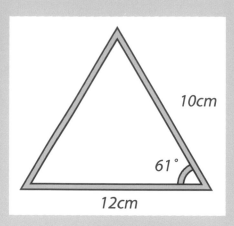

5. Find the area of the triangle:

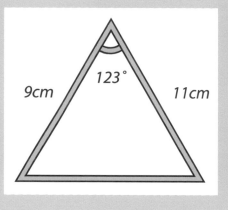

Section 5 – Using Algebra

Sequences

These questions are likely to give you a sequence and ask you to use a formula to find the nth term of the sequence. This formula allows you to put in different values of n to then find the number in the sequence for each term.

In order to find the formula, start by finding the difference between each number in the sequence.

For example:

Sequence   3   7   11   15   19   23

Difference   4   4   4   4   4

The difference between each number in the sequence is 4 each time.

Where the difference is the same after one line you need to remember the following formula:

$$Un = an + b$$

You can remember this as 'U Nan + Bob'

Un = the number that appears in the sequence
a = difference between the numbers in the sequence
n = n^{th} term
b = constant (this will be the same each time)

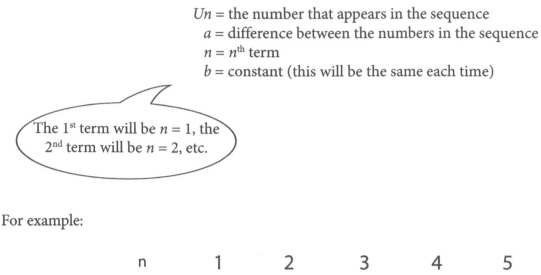

The 1st term will be $n = 1$, the 2nd term will be $n = 2$, etc.

For example:

n	1	2	3	4	5
Un	3	7	11	15	19
a		4	4	4	4

By remembering 'nuna' it will ensure you label the lines correctly. If you were to label the lines incorrectly it would spell something different.

So when $n = 1$, $Un = 3$, when $n = 2$, $Un = 7$, when $n = 3$, $Un = 11$, etc.

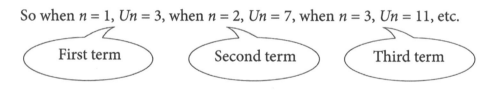

First term   Second term   Third term

The difference is 4 ($a = 4$), using the formula:

$$3 = 4(1) + b$$
$$3 = 4 + b$$
$$3 - 4 = b$$
$$b = -1$$

Double check this with a second pair:

$$7 = 4(2) + b$$
$$7 = 8 + b$$
$$7 - 8 = b$$
$$b = -1$$

As 'n' and 'Un' are constantly changing within the sequence, these will remain within the formula.

The 'a' and 'b' value will be the same for the sequence so these can be put into the formula:

$$Un = 4n - 1$$

This formula can help you find any of the sequence numbers.

For example:

If you needed to know the 100th term in the sequence you would use $n = 100$.

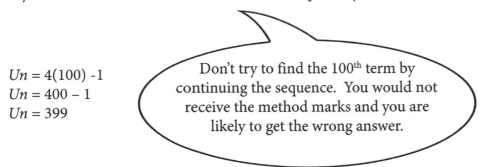

$Un = 4(100) -1$
$Un = 400 - 1$
$Un = 399$

Don't try to find the 100th term by continuing the sequence. You would not receive the method marks and you are likely to get the wrong answer.

What if the sequence does not have the same difference originally?

This difference may not be the same but the gap between each difference may eventually become the same.

For example:

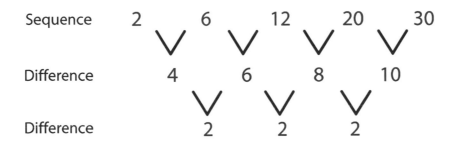

When it takes two lines in order for the difference to be the same use the formula:

$$Un = n^2 + b$$

The 'n' and 'Un' still represent the nth term and the sequence number, the only difference is that 'n' is squared and you don't need to use the difference. You need to work out how many lines it takes to get the same difference, but only so you can use the correct formula.

As before take 'pairs' from the sequence and place them into the formula. You can then rearrange to find b.

For example:

When $n = 1$, $Un = 2$, when $n = 2$, $Un = 6$, when $n = 3$, $Un = 12$, etc.

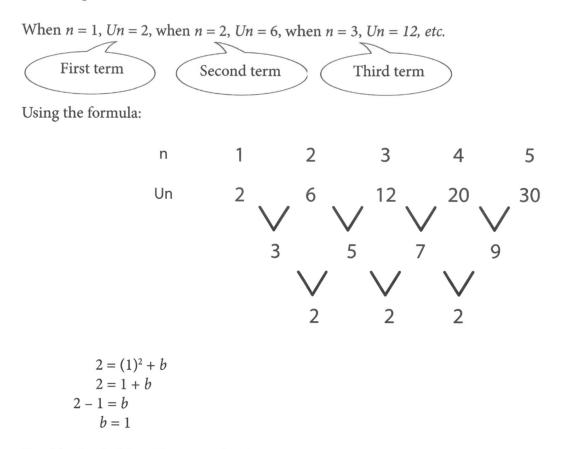

First term   Second term   Third term

Using the formula:

$$2 = (1)^2 + b$$
$$2 = 1 + b$$
$$2 - 1 = b$$
$$b = 1$$

Double check this with a second pair:

$$6 = (2)^2 + b$$
$$6 = 4 + b$$
$$6 - 4 = b$$
$$b = 2$$

The constant should always be the same value, so if it changes it must relate to the value of n.

When $n = 1$, $b = 1$
When $n = 2$, $b = 2$

The formula is therefore:

$$\boldsymbol{Un = n^2 + n}$$

Test this by replacing $n = 5$ into the formula as the value should be 30:

$Un = 5^2 + 5$
$Un = 25 + 5$
$Un = 30$

Now try these:

1. Using a formula, find the 50th term in the sequence 6, 13, 20, 27, 34, etc.

2. Using a formula, find the 85th term in the sequence 2, 5, 10, 17, 26, etc.

3. Find the nth term of the sequence 5, -3, -11, -19, -27, etc.

Distance, Speed & Time

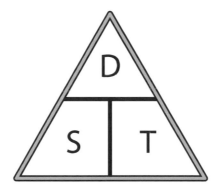

Remember, the letters are in alphabetical order.

So....

Distance = Speed x Time
   Speed = Distance ÷ Time
    Time = Distance ÷ Speed

For example:

If a person runs 200m in 30 seconds, what is their speed?

Speed = $\dfrac{200m}{30\sec s}$ Speed = 6.6mps

For example:

If a car is travelling at 40mph over a distance of 103 miles, how long will this take?

$$\text{Time} = \frac{103 miles}{40 mph}$$

= 2.575 hours

Remember, this is not 2 hours 58 minutes, it is 2 hours and 0.575 of an hour which is 34.5 minutes.

Units

You need to be careful of the units as the speed measurement should represent the distance and time measurement. For example, if you had a speed in miles per hour, it shows that the distance is measured in miles and the time is measured in hours. If you were asked to find the speed you would need to enter the distance and time in the correct units.

For example:

If a person runs 5km in half an hour, what is their speed in metres per minute?

To solve this you need to change the distance into metres, which will be 5000m and the time in minutes which would be 30 minutes.

The speed is therefore $\frac{5000m}{30 min}$ = 166.67 metres per minute.

There are two types of travel graphs:

Distance/Time

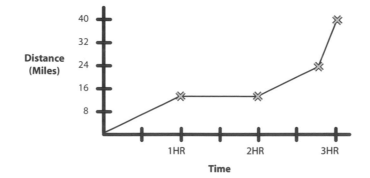

- A straight line means at a rest.
- A steeper line means the object is moving faster.
- These usually start from zero.

Looking at the graph above you can see that the object is travelling at a constant speed for the first hour for 16 miles but then rests for an hour. It then sets off again for another 8 miles and the last 16 miles of journey are much faster.

Speed/Time

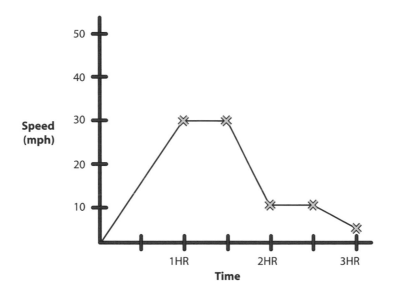

- A straight line means constant speed.
- A positive correlation line means acceleration.
- A negative correlation line means deceleration.

Looking at the graph above you can see an increase in speed for the first hour, it then stays constant for half an hour, decreases speed for next half an hour, has a constant speed again but then decreases to zero.

Now try these:

1. If a person runs at a speed of 9km/hr for 40 minutes, how far do they travel?

2. If a lorry travels for 3 hours and travels 150 miles what is the lorry's speed in miles per hour?

3. If a cyclist cycles for 20 minutes at a speed of 24km/hr, how far do they travel?

4. Describe the journey of the person which is shown in the distance/time graph below:

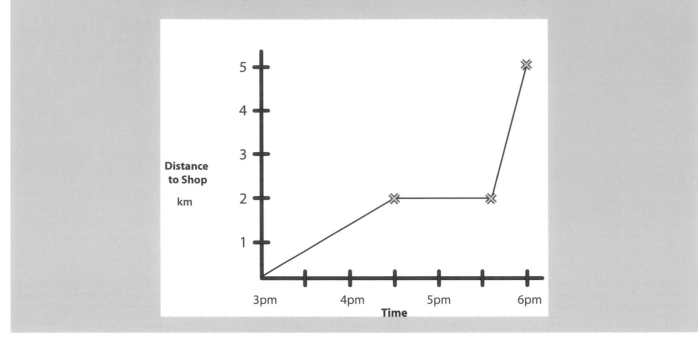

Mass, Density & Volume

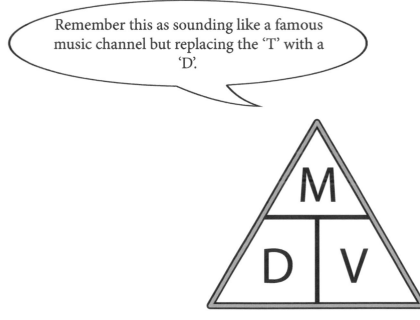

Remember this as sounding like a famous music channel but replacing the 'T' with a 'D'.

So:

Mass = Density x Volume
Density = Mass ÷ Volume
Volume = Mass ÷ Density

For example:

If a block of wood has a volume of 108cm³, find the mass if the density is 3g/cm³.

Mass = Density x Volume
Mass = 3g/cm³ x 108cm³
Mass = 324g

Now try these:

1. Find the density of a slab of metal if it weighs 500g and has a volume of 25cm³.

2. Find the volume of a brick if the mass is 1kg and the density is 25g/cm³.

Conversions

You need to be aware of the number of centimetres in a metre, pounds in a kilogram, etc. Therefore make sure you remember the following:

> 1 centimetre = 10 millimetres
>
> 1 metre = 100 centimetres
>
> 1 kilometre = 1000 metres
>
> 1 inch = 2.54 centimetres
>
> 1 foot ≈ 30 centimetres
>
> 1 mile ≈ 1.6 kilometres
>
> 1 litre ≈ 1.75 pints
>
> 1 gallon ≈ 4.5 litres

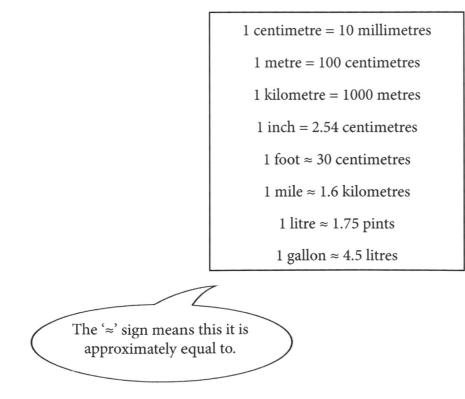

The '≈' sign means this it is approximately equal to.

You may be asked to convert one unit into another. You need to be aware of these in case the units need to be changed before you do any distance, speed and time calculations.

Currency is another way that conversions may be tested.

You could be asked to convert money where you are given the conversion rate. For example if £1 = $1.60, convert pounds into dollars and vice versa.

This is also very helpful for if you travel abroad. You don't want to be short changed.

For example:

How much is £66 in dollars?

If you know that £1 = $1.60
£66 = $1.60 x 66
= $105.60

If you know that £1 = $1.60, you can also convert dollars into pounds.

For example:

How much is $350 in pounds?

$350 into pounds, you need to work backwards.

If £1 = $1.60 rearrange to get $1 on its own:

$$\frac{£1}{1.60} = \$1$$

Once you know what $1 is, multiply this by the 350 to get the total for $350.

$$\frac{£1}{1.60} \times 350 = \$1 \times 350$$

£218.75 = $350

Watch out for these questions as they are not necessarily about currency but are very similar.

For example:

If £10,000 invested could give you 7 possible wins. How many wins would you expect if you invested £16,450?

$$£10,000 = 7 \text{ wins}$$

If £10,000 equates to 7 wins, you can rearrange this to find out what £1 will give you then multiply this amount by £16,450.

$$£1 = \frac{7 \text{ wins}}{10,000}$$

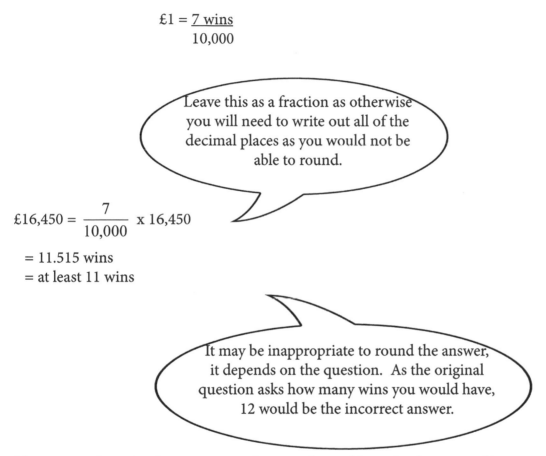

Leave this as a fraction as otherwise you will need to write out all of the decimal places as you would not be able to round.

$$£16,450 = \frac{7}{10,000} \times 16,450$$

= 11.515 wins
= at least 11 wins

It may be inappropriate to round the answer, it depends on the question. As the original question asks how many wins you would have, 12 would be the incorrect answer.

If you wanted to win about 17 times, how much would need to be invested?

$$£10,000 = 7 \text{ wins}$$

$$\frac{10,000}{7} = 1 \text{ win}$$

$$\frac{10,000}{7} \times 17 = 17 \text{ wins}$$

$$£24,285.71 = 17 \text{ wins}$$

This area may be tested using recipes.

For example:

The recipe for a cake which serves four people is:

> **200g Flour**
>
> **2 Eggs**
>
> **150g Caster Sugar**
>
> **100g Margarine**

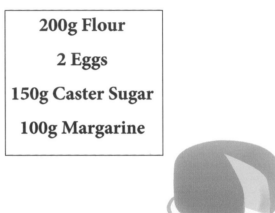

If you were asked to find the amount of ingredients needed for 11 people, firstly find the amounts for one person and then multiply by 11:

200g Flour ÷ 4 = 50g x 11 = 550g flour
2 Eggs ÷ 4 = 0.5 eggs x 11 = 5 ½ eggs
150g Caster Sugar ÷ 4 = 37.5g x 11 = 412.5g Caster Sugar
100g Margarine ÷ 4 = 25g x 11 = 275g Margarine

Now try these:

1. If the exchange rate is £1 = 1.20€, convert 465€ into pounds.

2. If the following recipe makes tomato soup for 6 people, how much of each ingredient would be required for 9 people?

    1.5kg tomatoes

    1.2 litres of boiling water

    2 tsp of tomato puree

    2 stock cubes

3. How many pints are in 2 litres?

4. If £450 buys 167 shares, how much would you need to spend to get 100 shares?

Section 6 – Angles & Transformations

Types of Angles

It is important that you remember the four main types of angles.

Acute

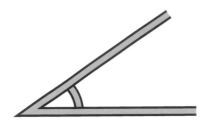

An acute angle is an angle which is less than 90º.

Right angled

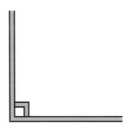

A right angle is exactly 90º.

Obtuse

An obtuse angle is angle which is more than 90º but less than 180º.

Reflex

A reflex angle can be anything from 180º up to 360º.
Most people know that the right angled triangle is a 90º angle, but mix up the other angles.

It helps to remember that when the angles are in alphabetical order, they go from the smaller angles to the larger angles.

A – Acute (up to 90º)
O – Obtuse (> 90º, < 180º)
R – Reflex (≥ 180º, < 360°)

Whenever you are given angles where a parallel line exists you will be finding either corresponding or alternate angles.

Corresponding

Corresponding angles are angles that appear again as if they had been copied. This can be checked using tracing paper.

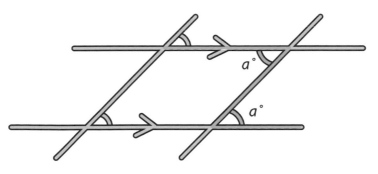

Alternate

Alternate angles exist where you can make a 'z' within the parallel angles. The two angles within the 'z' are the same and are known as alternate angles.

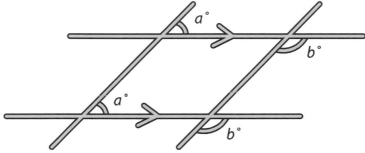

Interior

There are some exam questions which will require you to find the missing angles within a polygon (a shape). These angles are usually the same, so you just need to know what the total of the angles is within the shape. Let's think of some shapes:

Triangle   3 sides $180°$
Quadrilateral   4 sides $360°$

As you can see, for every side you add on to a shape, you can also add another $180°$.

For example:

5 sided shape	$540°$
6 sided shape	$720°$
7 sided shape	$900°$
8 sided shape	$1080°$

A typical exam question could be as follows:

Find x

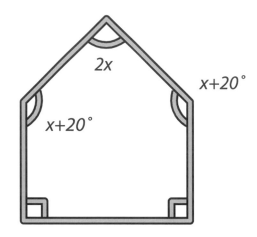

$$90° + 90° + x + 20° + 20° + x + 2x = 540°$$
$$220° + 4x = 540°$$
$$4x = 540° - 220°$$
$$4x = 320°$$
$$x = 320° \div 4$$
$$x = 80°$$

Exterior

Exterior angles are calculated based on the principle that each point has $360°$. If you know the interior angle, you are then able to calculate the exterior angle.

For example:

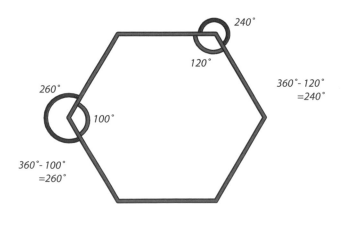

Now try these:

1. Find the value of angle a

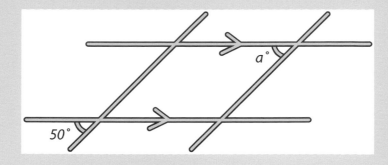

2. Find the value of angle b

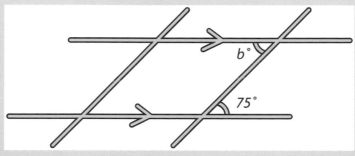

3. Find the value of angle r

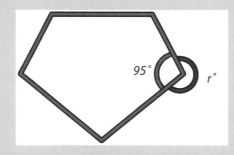

4. Find the value of x

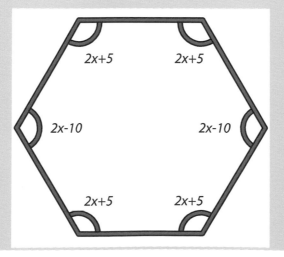

Angle Properties of Circles

You should familiarise yourself with the rules associated with angles within a circle, as these can be very easy marks once you've recognised what needs to be done.

Quadrilateral inside the circle

Where there is a quadrilateral inside the circle the opposite angles will add up to 180°.

For example:

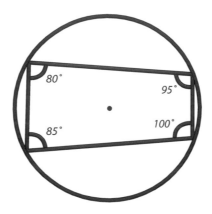

Angles in the centre and also touching circumference

Where there is an angle in the centre and also pointing in an arrow to the circumference, the angle in the centre is double the angle in the point.

For example:

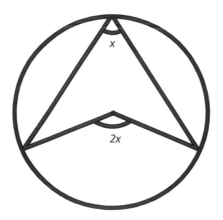

Tangents

A tangent is a straight line which runs outside the circle and touches it at one point.

The tangent is perpendicular to the radius where the tangent touches the circle.

For example:

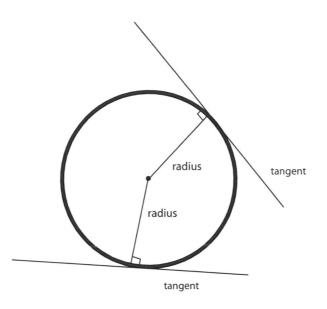

Where the tangents go to the circle from an external point, they are an equal length.

For example:

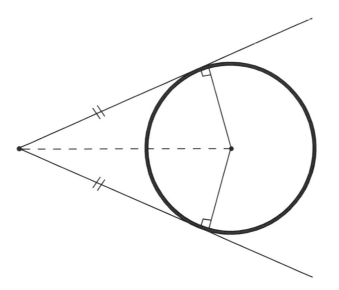

Now try these:

1. Find the value of *y*

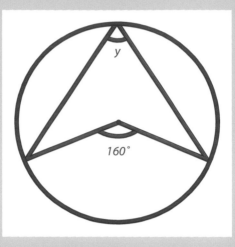

2. Find the value of *t*

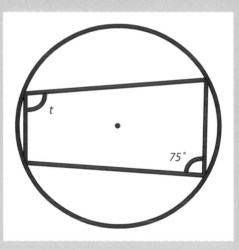

Transformations

Reflection

When reflecting a shape, imagine being in front of a mirror and how it would appear in the reflection. The reflection should be the same distance away from the lines on both sides as if it has been flipped over the line.

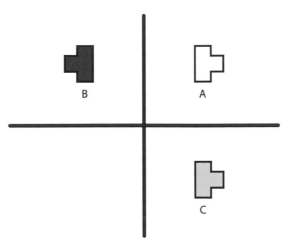

This will not necessarily be reflected in the x or y axis but could be a line where you are told the value of the line.

For example:

A reflection in the line $x = 3$ will be the line where the x value is always 3 but the y value changes.

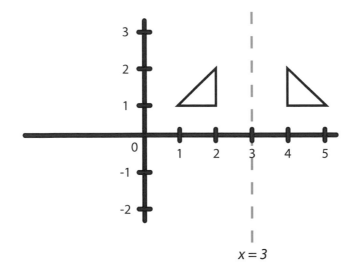

It could also be a reflection in the line $x = y$ which a diagonal line going through (0,0), (1,1), (2,2), etc. This is because the x value is the same as the y value.

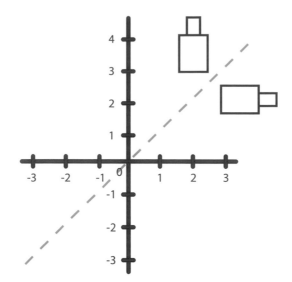

Rotation

It is best to use tracing paper if you are asked to rotate a shape. Even if it is not supplied in an exam you should be able to request it.

Mark a vertical line on the shape at 'o'clock' then move the shape and use this line to guide you when rotating.

Always rotate at a point on the grid and you will be given the coordinates. You can then use the point to twist the tracing paper around. For every 90° that it moves, move the vertical line around a quarter. The rotation direction is also very important and you will be told if it is anti-clockwise.

The direction will be clockwise unless the question states otherwise.

If the shape is moved 90° clockwise, the shape will be rotated forwards so the vertical line is at 'quarter past'. If it was moved anti clockwise 90° it will be at 'quarter to'.

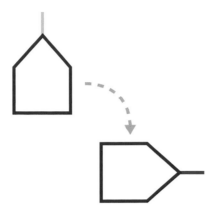

As you can see from the diagram below, if shape A is rotated in the point (0,0) the possible positions of 'A' are shown.

'A' rotated 90˚
anti clockwise at (0,0)

A

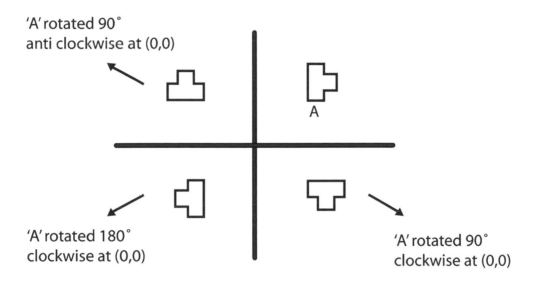

'A' rotated 180˚
clockwise at (0,0)

'A' rotated 90˚
clockwise at (0,0)

Translation

Translation means to move a shape either horizontally, vertically or both of these. As the shape will not move in any other direction it could be compared to the rook on a chess board.

For example:

If the translation is (7,-4), it means each points of the shape are moved across by 7 units and down by 4 units. You can then draw the shape in the new place on the grid.

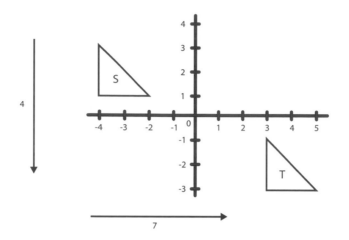

Enlargement

If you are asked to enlarge a shape you will be given a scale factor to enlarge this by. The scale factor represents how many times you enlarge the shape.

For example:

A scale factor 2 would change a shape as shown below:

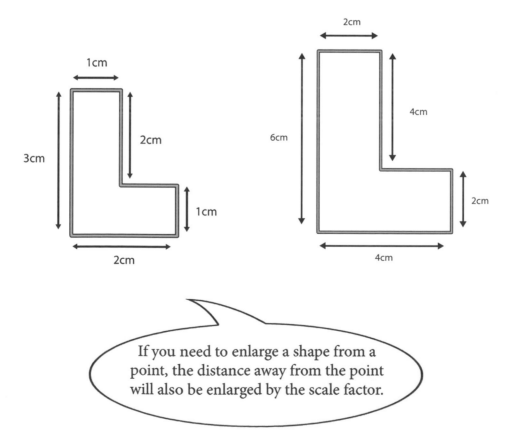

Tessellation

To show tessellation of shapes you need to slot shapes together. You should not need to rotate these shapes, they should hopefully slot together as they are.

For example:

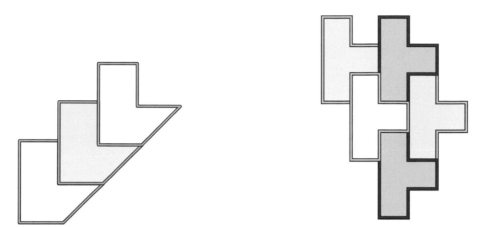

Now try these:

1. Describe the single transformation that makes shape A become shape B.

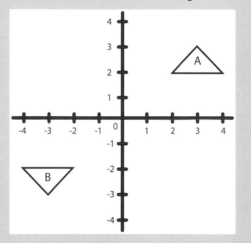

2. Describe the single transformation that makes shape C become shape D.

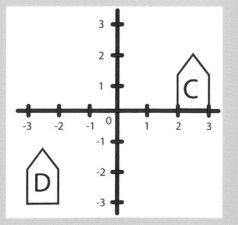

Symmetry

Symmetry may be tested in three different ways.

Line Symmetry

The best way to think of line symmetry is to imagine the shape folded in half. If it could be folded in half so the two halves are identical, the shape is symmetrical.

For example:

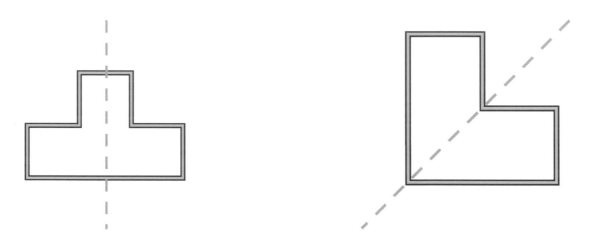

Plane of Symmetry

A plane of symmetry is similar to a line but this is when a solid shape is effectively cut into two equal halves.

For example:

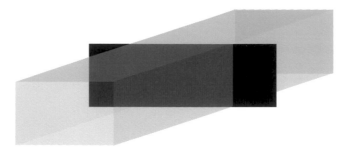

Rotational Symmetry

A shape is rotated from the centre and you can see how many times it would fit back into itself. The number of times that you are able to turn it back into the original position determines the 'order of rotational symmetry'.

The shape below would have rotational symmetry of order 1 as it does not go into the original position when rotated at all.

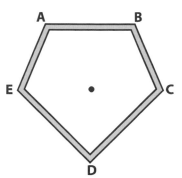

However, a rectangle would have rotational symmetry of order 2 as shown below:

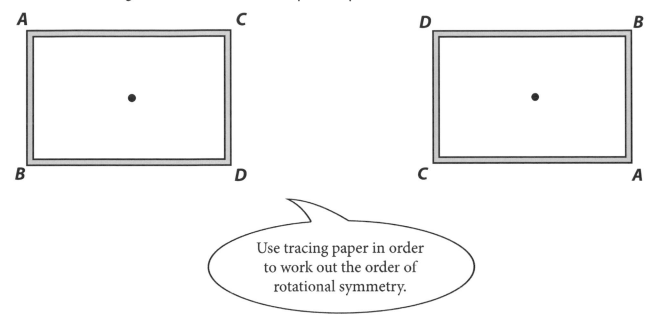

Use tracing paper in order to work out the order of rotational symmetry.

Now try these:

1. What would the order of rotational symmetry be for a square?

2. How many lines of symmetry does a square have?

3. How many lines of symmetry does a rectangle have?

Bearings

Bearings are all written as a three figure number. So a captain of a ship will always give the full three digits even when there is a zero.

Eg. 003°, 067°, 020°, 123°, etc......

For example:

If asked to take a bearing of A from B, you take it <u>from</u> B.
If asked to take a bearing of B from A, you take it <u>from</u> A.

<u>Step1</u>
Draw a dotted line between two points.

<u>Step 2</u>
Put a 'north flag' on the point you are taking the bearing from.

<u>Step 3</u>
Draw the angle in from the flag, clockwise until you reach the dotted line.

<u>Step 4</u>
Measure the angle.

For example:

Find bearing of A from B

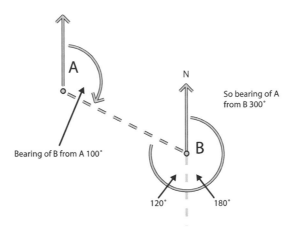

Bearing of B from A 100°

So bearing of A from B 300°

120°   180°

The semi circle will be 180°, so if you are measuring the rest using a protractor, there is an additional 120°. Adding both parts together gives a total of 300°.

Now try these:

1. Find the bearing of C from D

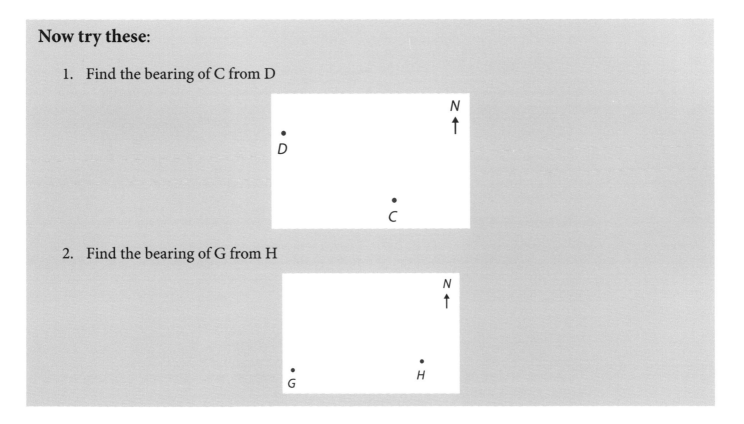

2. Find the bearing of G from H

Loci

The locus of points means possible points. You may be asked the possible points that lie from points or even lines. You are effectively drawing a border around the point/line but the border must be the correct distance all the way around.

If there is a box and need to show the locus of points 1cm away from the box, you would expect it to look like this:

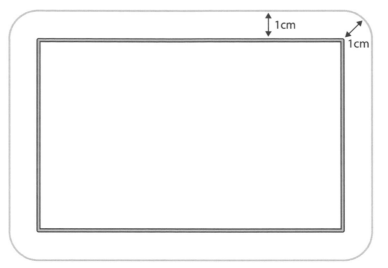

Where you have a line, draw a parallel line. Where you have a point, draw a curve with a compass.

Think about this logically, if you drew a larger box around the outside of the box the corners would not be correct. The distance would be longer from the corner from the smaller box to the corner of the larger box proven by Pythagorus Theorem. This is why a compass should be used for the points as this ensures that the distance is the same from a point.

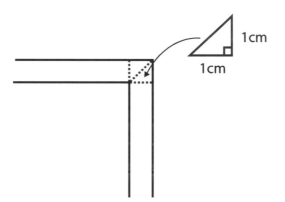

Equidistance

If the question asks you to find the equidistance between two points it is the equal distance. When points are exactly the same distance away from a point/line it needs to be shown in a particular way. Do not use a ruler and measure, even if this does give the correct answer. The equal distance needs to be found using a compass.

Use the compass to draw a circle from each point, keeping the size of the circle exactly the same for both points. Do not change the gap on the compass.

Where the circles overlap, draw a line between the two points. The line will then represent the equidistance and points on the line would be the locus of points.

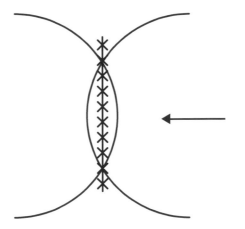

The question may ask you to mark on a map the locus of points when told that they are equidistance between two points.

For example:

An object has to be equidistance in a room between two walls. Find the locus of points for this object.

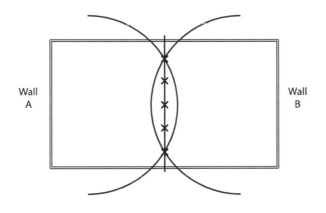

For example:

There is treasure on an island, equidistance between the hut and the tree. It is also 7km from the lake. Show the locus of points for the treasure.

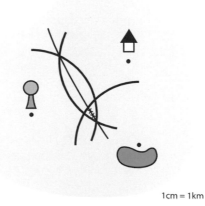

1cm = 1km

Now try these:

1. Show the locus of points of a printer that has to be 5km from the electricity supply (point A) and equidistance between the computers.

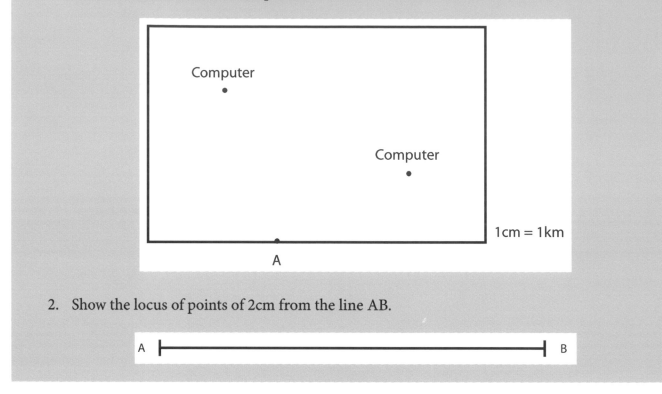

2. Show the locus of points of 2cm from the line AB.

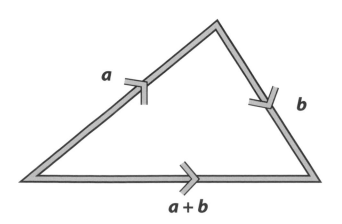

Vectors

A vector is a length which also has a direction. You will be aiming to reach a point and need to find a way to get to the point using the labelled sides.

Vectors can be written as bold letters or letters which are underlined. Please note that they do not have to be written in the order that you would do them in.

For example:

This could have also been written as <u>a</u> + <u>b</u> if the letters were not in bold or alternatively, **b** + **a**.

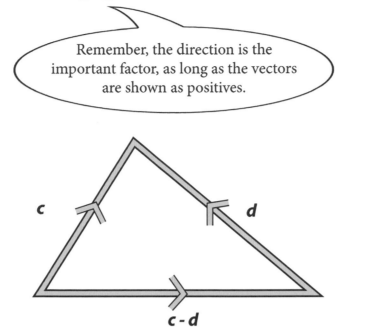

This may also been written as <u>c</u> – <u>d</u> if the letters were not in bold. Or alternatively written as – **d** + **c** although you should put a positive first if there is one.

Now try these:

1. Using the diagram below, find the single vector that represents the following paths:

a) *g – h*
b) *d + b*
c) *f + b*
d) *a – d*

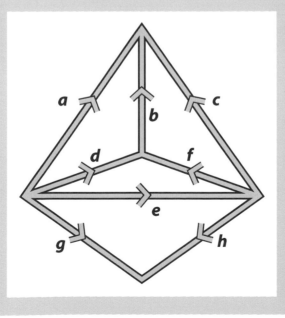

Section 7 - Graphs

The Basics

Before looking at graphs, you should make sure you understand the basic points.

The graph is made up of the x axis and the y axis as shown below:

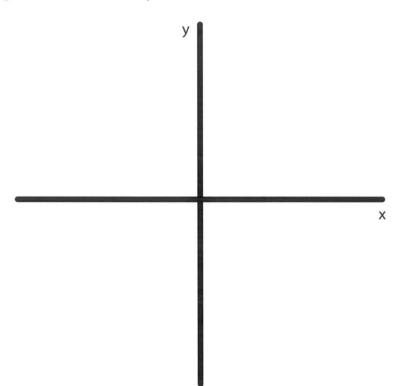

It is very important that you remember the difference between the two axes as this could lead to incorrect answers.

The x axis is the horizontal axis. Remember this by comparing x to a crab, which can stretch out horizontally.

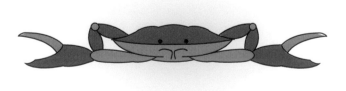

The *y* axis is the vertical axis which is taller and stretches out vertically. To remember this, imagine someone sitting on the tail of the *y* which pulls it down further and stretches it vertically.

Coordinates

When looking at graphs you may be asked to plot points which are given as coordinates. Coordinates are given in a bracket with the *x* value shown first, then the *y* value. Remember that this is always in alphabetical order (*x*, *y*).

For example:

A point plotted at (7, 2) shows the *x* value is 7 and the *y* value is 2.

A point plotted at (-1, 4) shows the *x* value is -1 and the *y* value is 4.

The coordinates can then be plotted on the axes as shown below.

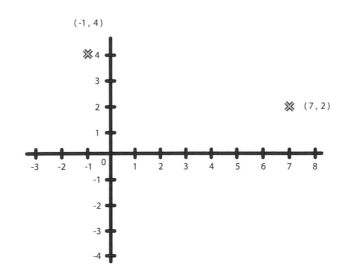

Now try these:

1) Find the coordinates of the points below:

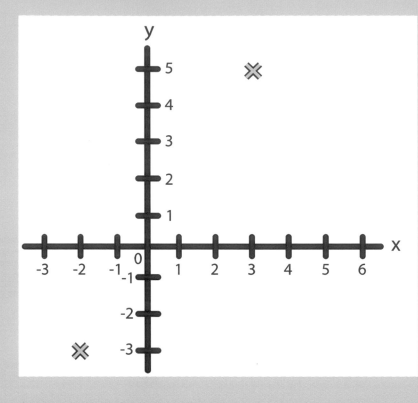

2) Plot the coordinates (5,2) and (4,-1) on an axes.

Linear Equations - Straight line graphs

An equation where the highest power of x is one is a linear equation.

For example:

$$y = 2x + 3$$
$$x = y - 7$$
$$9 = y + 3x$$

A linear equation is always in the following format:

$$y = mx + c$$

The linear equation represents a straight line where m is the gradient and c is where the line crosses the y axis. The x and y represent co-ordinates (x,y) which are on the straight line.

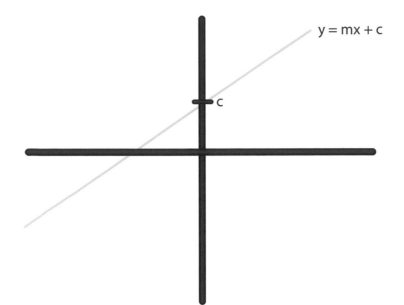

For example:

$y = 3x + 7$

This represents an equation where the gradient is 3 and the line crosses the y axis at 7.

$y = 2x - 3$

This represents an equation where the gradient is 2 and the line crosses the y axis at -3.

To read the gradient and the point where it crosses the y axis the equation must be equal to y. If the equation was $2y = 8x + 4$, you should divide by 2 to get y on its own.

For example:

$9 - 6y = 3x$
$-6y = 3x - 9$
$y = -0.5x + 1.5$

The gradient is -0.5 and the line will cross the y axis at 1.5.

A typical question will ask you to draw the straight line from an equation. Sometimes a table will be included for you to complete in order to work out the values. If there is no table you could always draw it in order to help you plot the graph.

For example:

$y = 2x + 5$

x	-3	-2	-1	0	1	2	3	4
y	-1	1	3	5	7	9	11	13

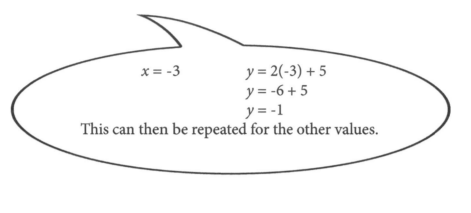

$x = -3$ $y = 2(-3) + 5$
$y = -6 + 5$
$y = -1$
This can then be repeated for the other values.

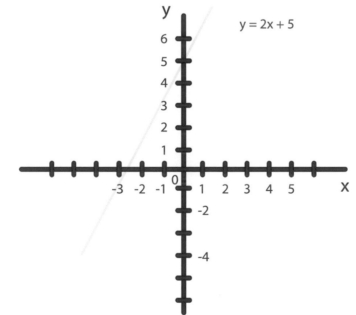

There is a way of sketching a graph without using the table. To find where the line crosses the x axis, replace $y = 0$ into the equation and rearrange to get x is on its own.

$0 = 2x + 5$

$-5 = 2x$

$\dfrac{-5}{2} = x$

Gradient

The direction of the line depends on the gradient (m).

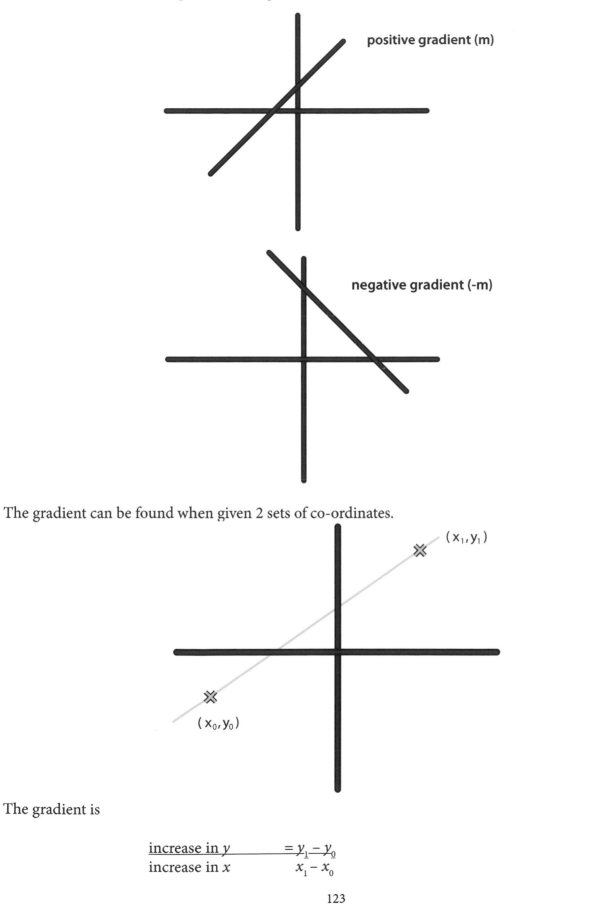

positive gradient (m)

negative gradient (-m)

The gradient can be found when given 2 sets of co-ordinates.

(x_1, y_1)

(x_0, y_0)

The gradient is

$$\frac{\text{increase in } y}{\text{increase in } x} = \frac{y_1 - y_0}{x_1 - x_0}$$

For example:

If there are two points (-3, -2), (1, 6) on a straight line graph the gradient of the graph can be found as follows:

$$\frac{-2-6}{-3-1} = \frac{-8}{-4} = 2 \qquad \text{Gradient} = 2$$

This can also be found by rearranging the equation to get m on its own when it is the only unknown.

When asked to find the equation of a line

Instead of sketching or drawing the line, you may be asked to find the equation of a line.

For example:

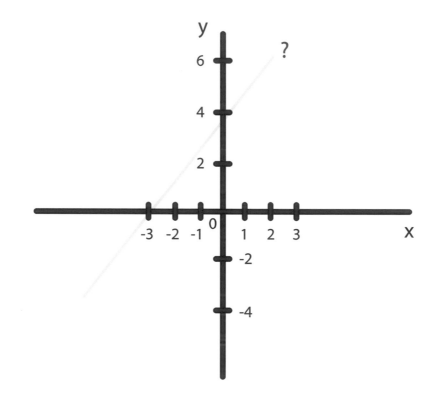

By looking at the equation you can see that $c = 4$, so $y = mx + 4$.

You need to find the gradient (m). As you can see where the line crosses both axes, you have two pairs of co-ordinates. You can find m by using one set of co-ordinates as it will be the only unknown and you can see what c is by the diagram.

$x = -3, y = 0$ $0 = -3m + 4$
                     $-4 = -3m$
                     $m = \dfrac{-4}{-3}$ $m = \dfrac{4}{3}$

Or you could do it using the equation:

Coordinates: (-3, 0) (0, 4)

$$\frac{4-0}{0--3} = \frac{4-0}{0+3} = \frac{4}{3}$$

Equation of line: $y = \frac{4}{3}x + 4$

Now try these:

1. Find the equation of the following line:

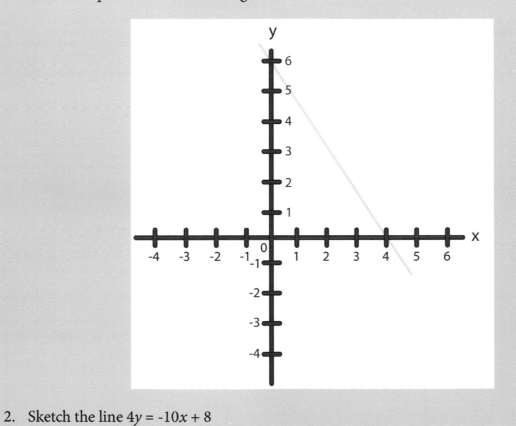

2. Sketch the line $4y = -10x + 8$

Scatter Graphs

A scatter graph compares two different variables. When values are plotted you can look at the spread of the points to determine whether or not there is a relationship between the two sets of results.

The plotted points on the scatter graph are sometimes in a general direction but this is not always the case. There are three main types of correlation that can be shown when the points are plotted:

No correlation

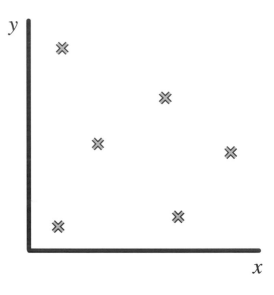

This is where there is absolutely no correlation between two factors. An example of this could be how tall you are and the results you get on a Maths test. The result of one of these factors has absolutely nothing to do with the other.

Positive correlation

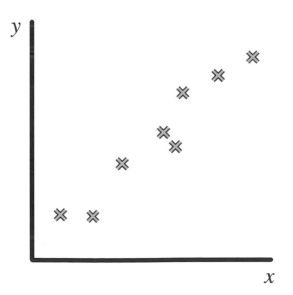

A positive correlation is the same direction as the positive gradient that you saw in the linear equation chapter. As one of the factors increases, the other factor also increases. A good example of this is the amount of rainfall and the depth of a lake during a certain period of time.

Negative correlation

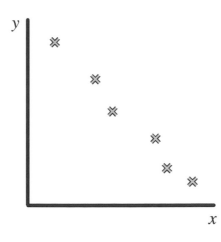

A negative correlation is the same direction as the negative gradient for linear equations. This is produced when the value of one factor increases as the other decreases. A good example of a negative correlation could be the age of a car and the value of the car.

Plotting a scatter graph

You may be asked to plot a scatter graph which only requires you to plot each point as a co-ordinate.

For example:

Draw a scatter graph to show the following information:

Age of computer (Years)	1	3	6	8	9
Value of computer (£)	£500	£300	100	50	25

The age and value are the two variables you will be plotting. One will be plotted on the x axis, the other on the y axis. It does not matter which way round they are plotted.

If you plot the age on the y axis and the value on the x axis, the graph will look like this:

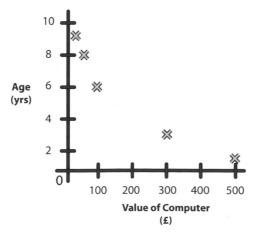

As you can see the points have been plotted as co-ordinates (500, 1), (300, 3), (100, 6), etc.

Line of best fit

If you are asked to draw a line of best fit, be careful as there is a certain way that this should be done. The line of best fit does not need to have an equal amount of points on both sides of the lines but it does need to show the direction of the line.

For example:

If you are given a scatter graph showing the following points, you would need to find the direction of the points and use a line to show this direction.

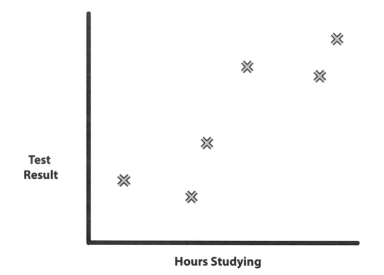

The line of best fit could look like this:

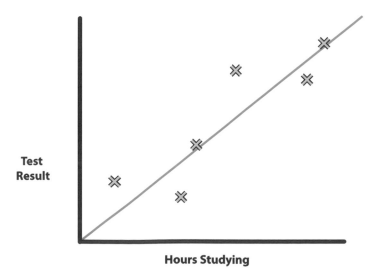

As you can see from the scatter graph, the line of best fit confirms that there is a positive correlation. You would expect this when looking at these two variables as the more studying you do, the higher the test result should be.

Obviously this is not always the case, which is shown by the points that are not on the line of best fit.

Now try these:

1. Draw the line of best fit for the following scatter graph:

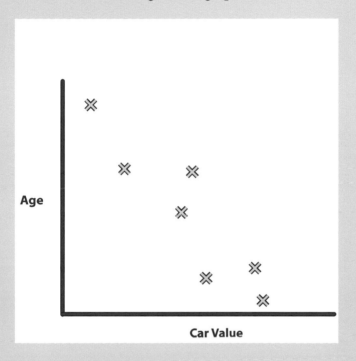

2. Draw a scatter graph to show the following information:

Height (cm)	170	154	190	161	185
Annual Salary (£'000)	20	30	12	40	35

3. Describe the correlation shown in the graphs in questions 1 and 2.

Solving Equations using Graphs

In the 'Quadratic' section you will see how to solve the quadratic equation and how it could be shown as a graph. When the equation is equal to zero, you can solve the equation by looking at the values where the graph crosses the x axis.

If the equation does not equal zero, rather than rearrange the equation and then have to solve it and sketch it again, there is a quicker way.

You only use the values where the graph crosses the x axis as this is the line where $y = 0$ which will be the case when the equation does equal zero. If this is not the case you can literally draw a line to show the value of y.

For example:

$y = x^3 + x^2 + x - 20$

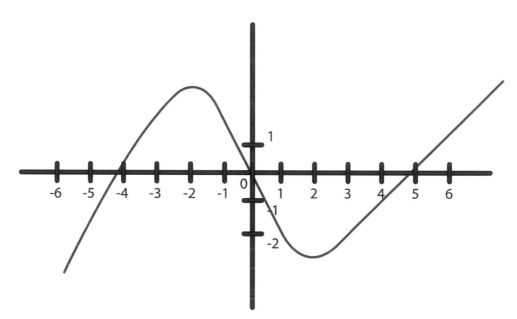

Solution of $x^3 + x^2 + x - 20 = 0$ will be:

$x = -4$ $\qquad\qquad$ $x = 0$ $\qquad\qquad$ $x = 5$

This is where the graph crosses at $y = 0$

You can add in additional lines if asked to solve an equation that does not equal zero.

For example:

$x^3 + x^2 + x - 20 = -2$ or $x^3 + x^2 + x - 20 = 1$.

This means you need to find solutions when $y = -2$ and $y = 1$. This requires you to draw a line across these points and read off the values.

For example:

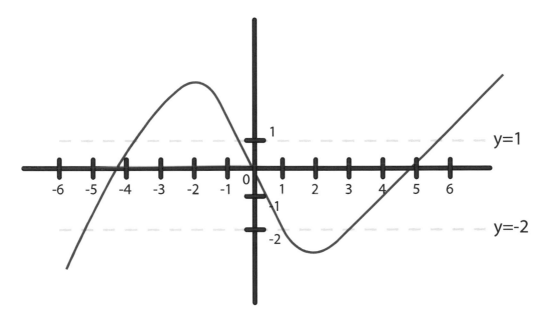

$x^3 + x^2 + x - 20 = -2$

From looking at the graph you can see that the values are as shown:

$x = -5.2$ $x = 1$ $x = 3$

$x^3 + x^2 + x - 20 = 1$

From looking at the graph you can see that the values are as shown:

$x = -3.8$ $x = -0.8$ $x = 5.7$

Now try these:

1. If the graph below represents the equation $y = x^3 + 4x^2 + x - 6$, solve the equation when $y = -1$.

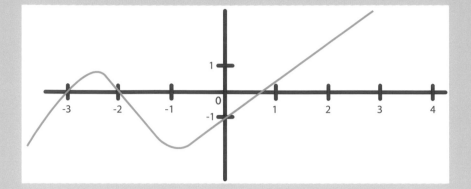

2. If the graph below represents the equation $y = x^3 - 5x^2 + 2x + 8$, solve the equation when $y = 1$.

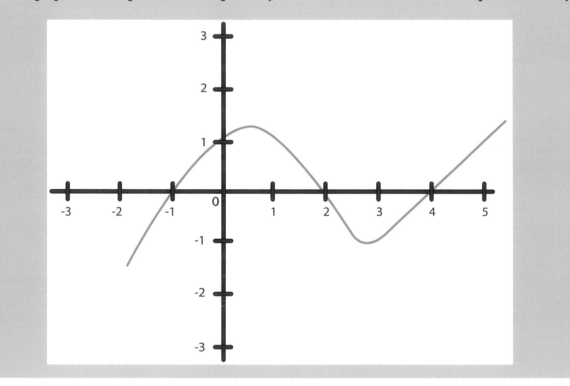

Graph Transformations

If $f(x)$ is a graph, transformations of the graph can be given by changing the $f(x)$. If '$f(x)$' remains unchanged, there is a change to the y co-ordinate. If there is an item in the bracket with the x, there is a change to the x co-ordinate.

Examples of when $f(x)$ remains unchanged:

$y = 3f(x)$
$y = f(x) + 4$
$y = -f(x)$

If the bracket becomes wider, it could look like any of the following:

$y = f(x - 4)$
$y = f(3x)$
$y = f(-x)$

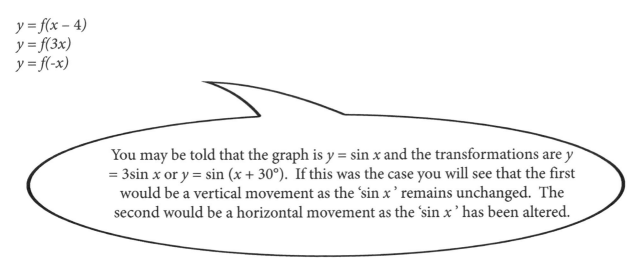

You may be told that the graph is $y = \sin x$ and the transformations are $y = 3\sin x$ or $y = \sin(x + 30°)$. If this was the case you will see that the first would be a vertical movement as the '$\sin x$' remains unchanged. The second would be a horizontal movement as the '$\sin x$' has been altered.

When the transformation is within the bracket it will do the opposite of what is shown. For example, $y = f(x + 2)$. This will move the graph horizontally back by 2. If $y = f(2x)$, the graph will be stretched horizontally by ½.

$-f(x)$

- This is a reflection in the x axis
- Only the y co-ordinate will change as the '$f(x)$' remains unchanged

$f(-x)$

- This is a reflection in the y axis
- Only the x co-ordinate will change as the original '$f(x)$' has been changed

$f(x) + a$

- Shift the graph vertically by 'a'
- Only the y co-ordinate will change as the original '$f(x)$' remains unchanged

$f(x + a)$

- Shift the graph horizontally by '$-a$'
- Only the x co-ordinate will change as the original '$f(x)$' has been changed

$af(x)$

- The graph is stretched vertically by 'a'
- Only the y co-ordinate will change as the original '$f(x)$' remains unchanged

$f(ax)$

- Stretch the graph horizontally by '$1/a$'
- Only the x co-ordinate will change as the original '$f(x)$' has been changed

You may be asked to sketch the revised graphs or possibly asked for the revised coordinates.

For example:

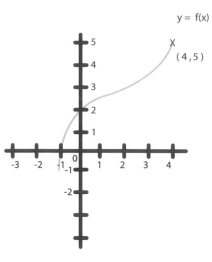

$y = f(x)$

If the diagram represents a graph $f(x)$ which ends at point X, the transformations below would produce the following coordinates:

$y = -f(x)$ X = (4, -5)

$y = f(-x)$ X = (-4, 5)

$y = f(x) + 2$ X = (4, 7)

$y = f(x - 3)$ X = (7, 5)

$y = 4f(x)$ X = (4, 20)

$y = f(2x)$ X = (2, 5)

Now try these:

1. Using the graph below:

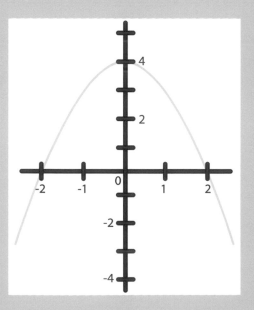

a) Sketch the revised graph if $y = f(x + 2)$

b) Sketch the revised graph if $y = 3f(x)$

134

Sine, Cosine and Tangent Graphs

You have already met sine, cosine and tangent, otherwise known as sin, cos and tan.

Although you will have previously used the calculator to find values of these functions, you also need to know the graphs. You may be asked to sketch these graphs so you need to remember some key points.

Sine Graph

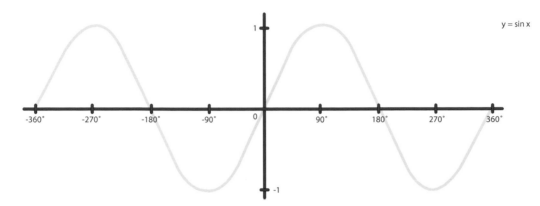

Looking at the graph above, it repeats every 360° and is in the shape of a backwards 'S' when you look at it from zero. The values of the sine graph vary between 1 and -1.

You can also find other values by deducting a value from 180°.

For example:

The values are the same for the following:

Sin 30° = Sin 150°
Sin 100° = Sin 80°
Sin -30° = Sin 210°

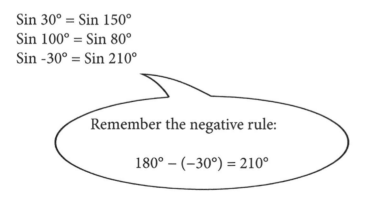

Remember the negative rule:

$$180° - (-30°) = 210°$$

Cosine Graph

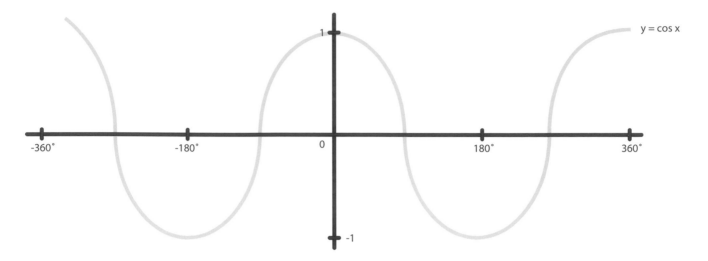

Take a look at the graph above, it repeats every 360° and is in the shape of a 'C' when you look at it from zero. The values of the cosine graph vary between 1 and -1.

You can also find the equivalent point on the graph by making the angle a negative.

For example:

The values are the same for the following:

Cos 40° = Cos -40°
Cos 65° = Cos -65°
Cos -120° = Cos 120°

Tangent Graph

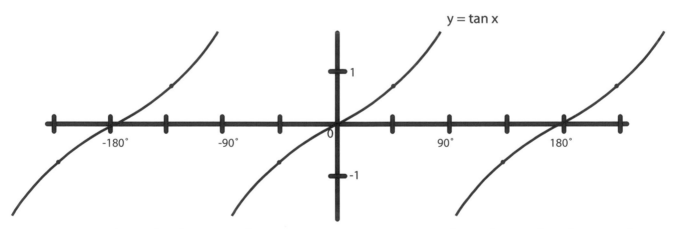

As you can see from the above graph, it repeats every 180°, goes through zero but does not have a minimum or maximum point.

Use your calculator to test the above graphs.

For example:

Sin 180° = 0
Cos 180° = -1
Tan 180° = 0
Sin 90° = 1
Cos 90° = 0

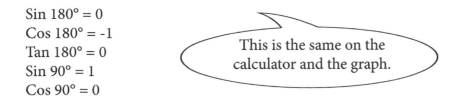

This is the same on the calculator and the graph.

Now try these:

1. Using the graphs, find the solutions to the following:

a) Cos -90°

b) Sin 270°

2. Using your knowledge from the graph transformation section, sketch the following graphs:

a) Sin 2x

b) 2Cos x

c) Sin(x – 30°)

Section 8 – Collecting and Representing Data

Collecting Data

Questionnaires

Questionnaires are a common method of collecting data. You may be asked to create a questionnaire. Remember to ask closed questions in the questionnaire so the answers are limited.

For example:

- Yes/No boxes
- Tick boxes

Tally Charts

The easiest way to collect data is to use a tally chart. You may be given a tally chart which you then have to work out the amount of results.

The key thing to remember about tally charts is that after every four results the fifth result goes through the four.

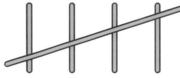

For example:

If 30 office workers were asked what they had to eat at lunchtime, the results can be shown in a tally chart.

If you were given the tally chart you could also work out the number of people for each type of lunch by counting the marks in the 'tally' column. By adding the frequency column you can create a frequency distribution:

Lunches	Tally	Frequency
Sandwiches	ⅢⅢ Ⅲ II	12
Salads	ⅢⅢ I	6
Soup	IIII	4
Other	ⅢⅢ III	8
		30

1. If you are given the following results in a tally chart, complete a frequency distribution to show the number of results for each type of journey.

Journey to Work	Tally	Frequency
Car	JHT JHT JHT	
Train	JHT II	
Bus	JHT JHT	
Walk	IIII	
Other	JHT JHT I	

Representing Data

When drawing a graph/chart, the graph/chart should always have a title so you can see what the data represents.

Pictograms

A pictogram is a way of representing data by using pictures to represent the frequency. A key is needed for a pictogram to determine how many results the object represents. You will not necessarily be given whole objects, you may be given half of the object, a quarter, etc.

For example:

Monday	🍾🍾
Tuesday	🍾🍾🍾
Wednesday	🍾🍾🍾
Thursday	🍾🍾🍾🍾🍾
Friday	🍾

Key: 🍾 = 10 sweets

Bar Charts

A bar chart is a popular way of representing data. The height of each bar represents the number of results, but the width of the bars is always the same. The bar chart is completely different to the histogram which you will see later in the chapter.

For example:

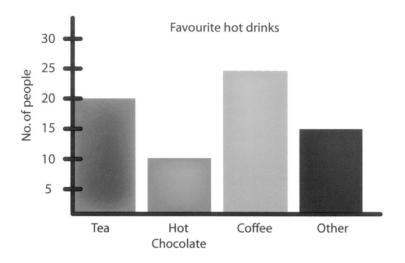

Stem and Leaf Diagram

The stem and leaf diagram is used to show data in the correct order from the smallest result to the largest result. The stem can represent units, tens, etc. The key will show what the stem represents and give an example of how the numbers are going to be made up.

For example:

If you had the following data it could be put into a stem and leaf diagram using units as the stem:
5.7, 1.6, 4.4, 3.7, 3.2, 5.6, 1.1, 1.9, 3.2, 4.8, 2.3, 2.4

Key: $1 \mid 0.1 = 1.1$

1	0.1	0.6	0.9
2	0.3	0.4	
3	0.2	0.2	0.7
4	0.4	0.8	
5	0.6	0.7	

The data in the stem and leaf diagram can then be used to find the mean, mode, median and range as shown in a later chapter.

Revisit this section once you have looked at the mean, mode, median and range method to make sure you feel comfortable calculating these from a stem and leaf diagram.

Line Graphs

A line graph is another graph which represents data, however straight lines are used to join the points for the results.

Remember, these are not plotted at the midpoint or upper limit, the amounts are plotted on the actual number.

For example:

If you were given the following results for the number of ice creams sold in different years, it could be shown in a line graph.

Year	Amount of ice creams sold
2003	63,000
2004	60,000
2005	52,000
2006	64,000
2007	76,000
2008	55,000

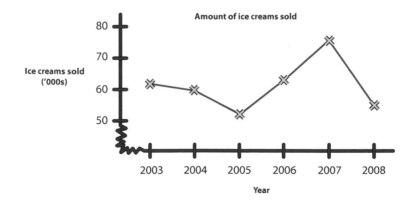

It is worth noting that you do not always have to write the full range of values. You can use a 'squiggle' in order to show that you are not including all the previous results.

The 'squiggle' was used in the line graph above.

Now try these:

1. Find the total number of results for each holiday destination given the pictogram below:

Spain	○ ○ ○
France	○ ○ (
Florida	○ ○ ○ ○ ○
Mexico	○ ○ ○ ○
Egypt	○ ○ ○ ○ ○ ○
Other	○ ○ ○

Key: ○ = 6 people

2. Using the stem and leaf diagram below, find the median, mode and range of the data.

Key: 1 | 2 = 12

1	2	3	4	
2	6	9		
3	1	4	7	7

3. Put the following results into a stem and leaf diagram using an appropriate key:

$$34, 76, 64, 35, 46, 56, 34, 41, 72, 68, 39$$

4. Use a line graph to show the following data:

Season	Average amount per household spent on flowers (£s)
Spring	44
Summer	80
Autumn	30
Winter	16

Pie charts

As you know there are 360° in a circle, you can split the 360° to represent results. This is how a pie chart is formed.

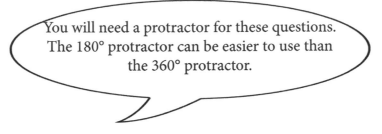

You will need a protractor for these questions. The 180° protractor can be easier to use than the 360° protractor.

Put the results as a fraction so that the 360° can then be split by this fraction. All the sectors should add back up to 360°.

For example:

Results	Frequency	Degrees in sector
$0< x \leq 10$	4	4/36 x 360° = 40°
$10< x \leq 20$	12	12/36 x 360° = 120°
$20< x \leq 30$	5	5/36 x 360° = 50°
$30< x \leq 40$	9	9/36 x 360° = 90°
$40< x \leq 50$	6	6/36 x 360° = 60°
	36	360°

You can also divide the 360° by the number of results. There will therefore be this many degrees per result, you can then multiply by the numbers of results. This is effectively the same thing as multiplying by the fraction.

For example:

Results	Frequency	Degrees in sector
$0 < x \leq 10$	4	$360° \div 36 = 10° \times 4 = 40°$
$10 < x \leq 20$	12	$360° \div 36 = 10° \times 12 = 120°$
$20 < x \leq 30$	5	$360° \div 36 = 10° \times 5 = 50°$
$30 < x \leq 40$	9	$360° \div 36 = 10° \times 9 = 90°$
$40 < x \leq 50$	6	$360° \div 36 = 10° \times 6 = 60°$
	36	$360°$

It's up to you which way you split the pie chart. As you can see from the table, both ways will produce the same answer.

The results on the tables shown would produce the following pie chart:

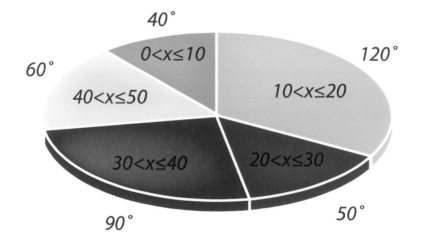

You may be given a pie chart and then have to find the number of results in each category.

For example:

24 people are surveyed about their favourite type of holiday and the following pie chart is produced:

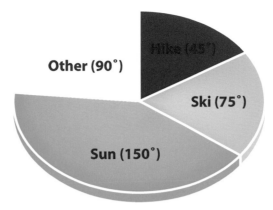

Work backwards to find out exactly how many people liked each type of holiday. Previously you divided each frequency by the total and multiplied by 360°.

Holiday	Frequency	Degrees in sector
Ski	?	?/24 x 360° = 75°
Hike	?	?/24 x 360° = 45°
Sun	?	?/24 x 360° = 150°
Other	?	?/24 x 360° = 90°
	24	360°

Using the rearranging rules, you can rearrange each sum:

$$\frac{x}{24} \times 360° = 75$$

$$\frac{x}{24} = 75° \div 360°$$

$$x = \frac{75}{360} \times 24$$

$$x = 5$$

By continuing with the other values you can see that three people preferred hiking, ten preferred the sun and six people preferred a different type of holiday.

Now try these:

1. Draw a pie chart to represent the following results:

Favourite colour	Frequency
Yellow	16
Red	22
Green	10
Blue	24
	72

2. Using the pie chart below, find the number of people for each type of pet if 36 people were surveyed.

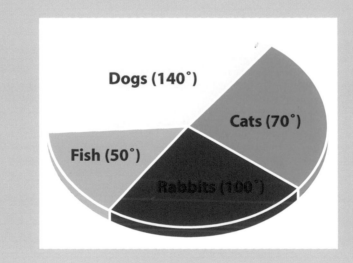

Histograms

If you see the word 'histogram' think of frequency density. Some people believe a histogram is a bar chart but this is not the case. The two are very different.

The main difference between a bar chart and a histogram is the bars of a histogram can be different widths. The height of the bars on a histogram depends on the frequency density of the group. The bars therefore show the frequency of the results rather than the height.

$$\text{Frequency density} = \frac{\text{Frequency}}{\text{Class Width}}$$

This effectively spreads the frequency depending on the class widths so it is the area of the bar that actually represents the frequency.

You may be given a chart showing the groups and the number of results in each group.

For example:

Scores	Frequency		
$0 \leq x \leq 15$	30		
$15 < x \leq 25$	20		
$25 < x \leq 40$	45		
$40 < x \leq 60$	20		

Remember, the histogram must show frequency density. You will therefore need to add two columns on the table to show 'class width' and the other to show 'frequency density'.

Scores	Frequency	Class Width	Frequency Density
$0 \leq x \leq 15$	30	15	2
$15 < x \leq 25$	20	10	2
$25 < x \leq 40$	45	15	3
$40 < x \leq 60$	20	20	1

It is then the frequency density which is plotted against the class widths so the histogram would look like this:

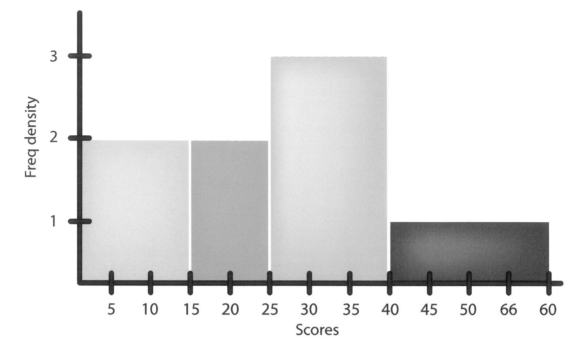

This may be tested backwards where you need to find the frequency but are given the histogram. This should not cause problems as long as you remember that the histogram plots the frequency density.

For example:

Find the number of results in each of the groups:

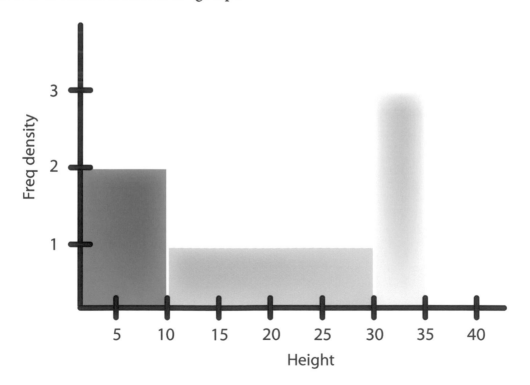

Based on the histogram you can produce the following table:

Height	Frequency Density	Class Width	Frequency
$0 \leq x \leq 10$	2	10	?
$10 < x \leq 30$	1	20	?
$30 < x \leq 35$	3	5	?

You previously saw the formula:

$$\text{Frequency Density} = \frac{\text{Frequency}}{\text{Class Width}}$$

This can be rearranged to get the 'Frequency' on its own by moving the 'Class Width' to the other side where it will become a multiply as it was previously dividing.

$$\text{Frequency density x Class Width} = \text{Frequency}$$

This formula enables you to complete the table below in order to find the missing frequency amounts:

Height	Frequency Density	Class Width	Frequency
$0 \leq x \leq 10$	2	10	20
$10 < x \leq 30$	1	20	20
$30 < x \leq 35$	3	5	15

The frequency density is shown correctly here as 20 results in a class width of 10 represents two results for in every gap of one. The frequency density for 20 results in a class width of 20 represents one result for every gap of one.

Now try these:

1. Draw the histogram represented by the following table:

Scores	Frequency
$0 \leq x \leq 5$	10
$5 < x \leq 15$	30
$15 < x \leq 30$	15

2. Find the number of results in each of the score groups shown in the histogram below:

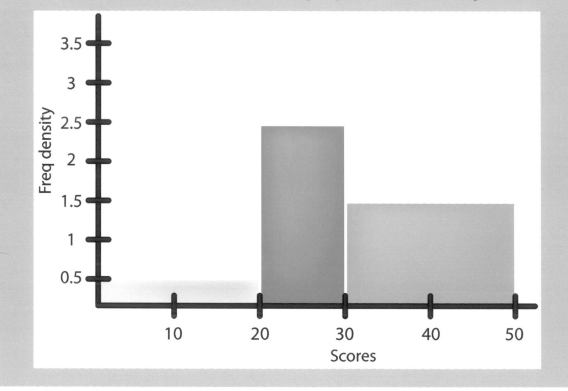

Frequency Polygons

Frequency polygons can be produced with the help of histograms or bar charts.

The points that are plotted are in the middle of the top of the bars produced for either the bar chart or histogram. These points are then joined with straight lines.

However, unlike line graphs, these points are joined to the x axis below the lowest value and above the highest value. Remember this by thinking of a lake. If you did not join the lines to the x axis, any water put in the lake would leak out.

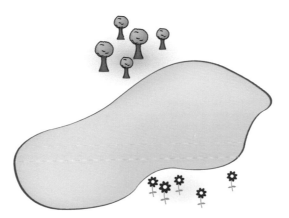

Looking at the histogram in the previous section, you can now draw a frequency polygon.

For example:

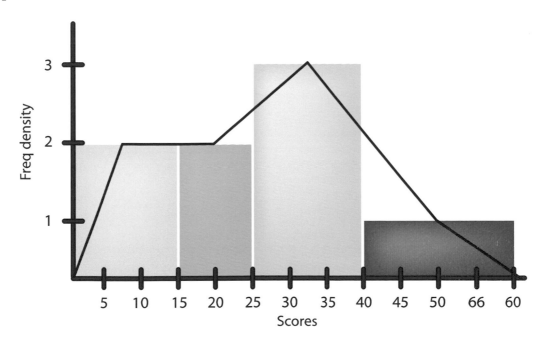

Now try these:

1. Draw the frequency polygon for the following histogram:

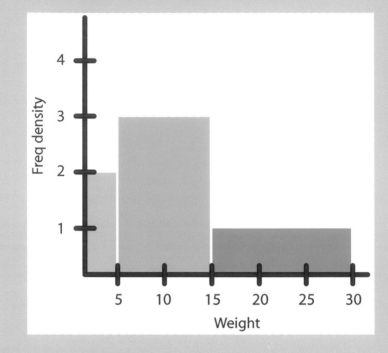

2. Draw the frequency polygon for the histogram shown below:

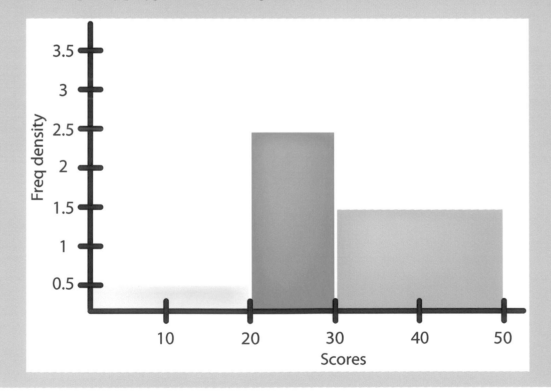

Section 9 – Analysing Data

Mean, Mode and Median – Single Data

Mean

If somebody is mean, they are not particularly nice. To find the mean, add all the results up and divide by the total number of results. This is not the easiest way of finding the average, hence why it is 'mean'.

Mode

The one that appears the most. 'The mode's the most', this can also be remembered as the word mode in French translates to fashion which is the most popular.

Median

Think of the middle of the Mediterranean Sea, middle of Med (very relaxing). If you are in the middle of the Mediterranean you will have gone from shallow water that gradually got deeper. The median is therefore in the middle of the numbers when they are in the correct order from smallest to largest.

If the middle has two numbers, an average needs to be taken of both numbers.

Range – The highest value less the smallest value. This should be an actual figure.

For example

Data: 4, 7, 2, 5, 7, 3, 9, 8, 1

Mode: 7 (appears the most)

Mean: 4 + 7 + 2 + 5 + 7 + 3 + 9 + 8 +1 = 46
         46 ÷ 9 = 5.11

Median: 1, 2, 3, 4, 5, 7, 7, 8, 9
         = 5

Range: 9 – 1 = 8

Now try these:

1. Find the mean, mode, median and range of the following data:

   4, 9, 6, 7, 5, 4, 2, 1, 3, 8

2. Find the mean, mode, median and range of the following data:

   56, 98, 76, 34, 61, 32, 98, 65, 45, 43, 11, 98

Cumulative Frequency

You may be asked to complete a cumulative frequency table and/or asked to draw a cumulative frequency graph.

When completing a table you will need to add the 'cumulative frequency column' to the table. Think of the word 'accumulate', this means to keep adding to something.   Cumulative is the same thing, you are adding up the frequencies as you go along. You are constantly looking at how many results from the lowest possible result to the top of each group.

For example:

In the second row you need to know how many results were between 0 and 10. This would be the 5 in between 0 and 5, then the 3 that are in between 5 and 10, so 8 in total.

Scores	Frequency	Cumulative Frequency
$0 \le x \le 5$	5	5
$5 < x \le 10$	3	8
$10 < x \le 15$	4	12
$15 < x \le 20$	8	20
Total	20	

You should always have the same amount at the end of the cumulative frequency column as the total results.

Cumulative Frequency Graphs

A cumulative frequency graph can be used to find the median with grouped data. The key point to remember is to use the graph to find the solution.

The graph needs to be plotted correctly, remember to plot the points at the upper limit of the group. You also need to remember that the graph is curvy (it does not have straight lines joining the separate points).

The graph will therefore look like this:

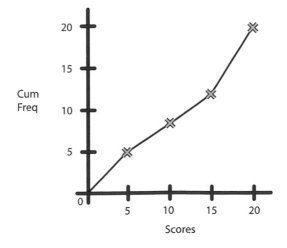

Now try these:

1. Draw a cumulative frequency graph to represent the data below:

Scores	Frequency
$0 \leq x \leq 10$	5
$10 < x \leq 20$	5
$20 < x \leq 30$	15
$30 < x \leq 40$	5
Total	30

2. Draw a cumulative frequency graph to represent the data below:

Scores	Frequency
$0 \leq x \leq 5$	10
$5 < x \leq 15$	5
$15 < x \leq 20$	10
$20 < x \leq 30$	5
Total	30

Mean & Mode - Grouped Data

It is not possible to find the mode for grouped data, instead you will find the modal class. This will be the group with the most results in it. Normally, you find the mean when the data is single numbers. However, it is possible to be given grouped data where a different method is required.

When given grouped data, it is impossible to know the actual numbers that were chosen. It is then necessary to change the group into a number that represents the group.

For example:

Assume that you are trying to calculate the mean score of 20 students taking an exam and you are told how many students scored between 0 to 5, 6 to 10, 11 to 15 and 16 to 20. This is represented by inequalities in a table which look like this:

Scores	Frequency		
$0 \leq x \leq 5$	5		
$5 < x \leq 10$	3		
$10 < x \leq 15$	4		
$15 < x \leq 20$	8		

As you do not know the actual values you cannot find the mean in the way we do for single data. You therefore need to find a number to represent the group. The number that will represent the group will be 'x', this will be the midpoint of the group. In order to calculate the midpoint, the upper limit of the group plus the lower limit of the group is divided by 2.

Scores	Frequency	x	
$0 \leq x \leq 5$	5	2.5	
$5 < x \leq 10$	3	7.5	
$10 < x \leq 15$	4	12.5	
$15 < x \leq 20$	8	17.5	

You can now ignore the first column and think about the data as single data. The above results show that the following results were scored:

2.5, 2.5, 2.5, 2.5, 2.5, 7.5, 7.5, 7.5, 12.5, 12.5, 12.5, 12.5, 17.5, 17.5, 17.5, 17.5, 17.5, 17.5, 17.5, 17.5.

By multiplying the 'frequency' and 'x' columns it is effectively the same as adding all of the results together. All of the 2.5s add up to 12.5, all the 7.5s to 22.5, all the 12.5s to 50 and the 17.5s add up to 140. The total of these numbers is 225 as shown in the table.

Scores	Frequency	x	fx
$0 \leq x \leq 5$	5	2.5	12.5
$5 < x \leq 10$	3	7.5	22.5
$10 < x \leq 15$	4	12.5	50
$15 < x \leq 20$	8	17.5	140
Total	20		225

Remember, the mean is the average so it's the total of all the numbers divided by how many there are. The 225 is therefore divided by the twenty different numbers, not the four different groups.

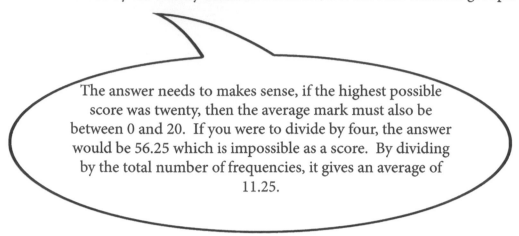

The answer needs to makes sense, if the highest possible score was twenty, then the average mark must also be between 0 and 20. If you were to divide by four, the answer would be 56.25 which is impossible as a score. By dividing by the total number of frequencies, it gives an average of 11.25.

Median & Interquartile Range

As shown previously, you are able to draw a cumulative frequency graph using grouped data. Using this graph you can find the median, lower quartile, upper quartile and interquartile range.

The lower quartile is the median of the lower half of the data and the upper quartile is the median of the upper quartile

In the previous section showing single data, you saw that the median is found in the middle of the results. With grouped data it is possible to work out what group this is, or use a cumulative frequency graph to find a more accurate result.

The median will be found at the middle result, the total results divided by 2. The middle result is where you will find the median but this is not the median.

The lower quartile will be found at the total results divided by 4. The first quarter is where you will find the lower quartile but this is not the lower quartile.

The upper quartile will be found at the total results multiplied by ¾. The third quarter is where you will find the upper quartile but this is not the upper quartile.

You can find the results by going across the graph and pulling the required numbers out of the bottom. Think of this as a vending machine, you put your coin in and get what you want out of the bottom. You find these amounts by going across to the graph and then the value you want falls out of the bottom of the graph.

When finding the median or quartiles be careful to apportion the number of results and not what the graph goes up to if you are reading the values from a cumulative frequency graph. The graph may go further than the total results.

Using our previously plotted cumulative frequency graph, you can find the median at 10, the lower quartile at 5 and the upper quartile at 15. The results are shown on the graph below.

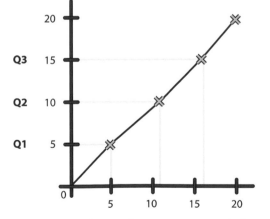

The interquartile range can also be found. This is the upper quartile less the lower quartile. This should never be a negative figure so if this is the case, the numbers were entered the wrong way round.

Now try these:

1. Find the median and interquartile range from the cumulative frequency graph below.

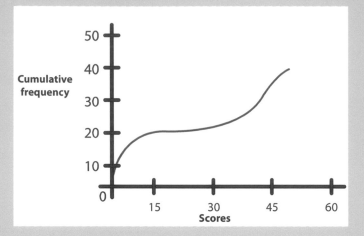

2. What is the interquartile range if the median is 35, the upper quartile is 50 and the lower quartile is 25?

Box Plots

Box plot diagrams are drawn to show the data from a cumulative frequency graph. They show the median, lower quartile, upper quartile, lowest possible value and highest possible value. They are sometimes called a box plot and whisker diagram.

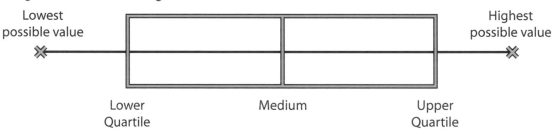

Refer to the previous cumulative frequency graph:

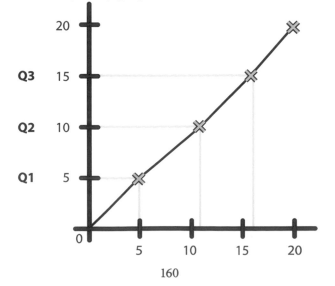

The information from the cumulative frequency graph can also be shown on a box plot diagram as shown below:

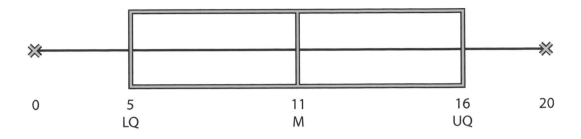

0	5	11	16	20
	LQ	M	UQ	

Now try these:

1. A class takes an exam which is out of 50 but the median result is 20. Show this information on a box plot diagram as well as the lower quartile of 10 and the upper quartile of 42.

2. Show the results for the following cumulative frequency graph on a box plot diagram.

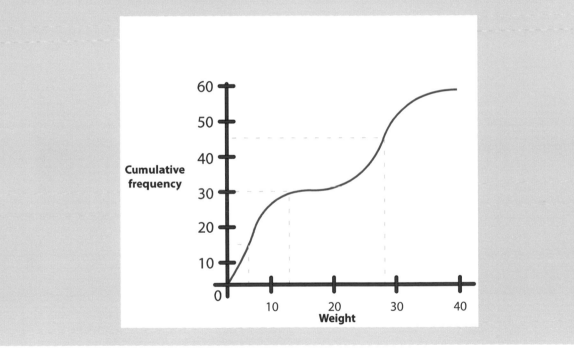

Moving Average

Moving averages can be used to find an average of different sets of data. The size of the data can vary.

A three point moving average covers an average of three results, a five point moving average covers five results, and so on.

It is called a moving average as the average is continuously taken through the set of data.

For example:

The table below shows the number of tourists who visit a seaside resort each year.

Year	2001	2002	2003	2004	2005	2006	2007	2008
Number of people	36,000	41,000	55,000	59,000	66,000	70,000	72,500	78,000

If you are asked for a three point moving average, take the average of three sets of results at a time but keep moving the three though the data.

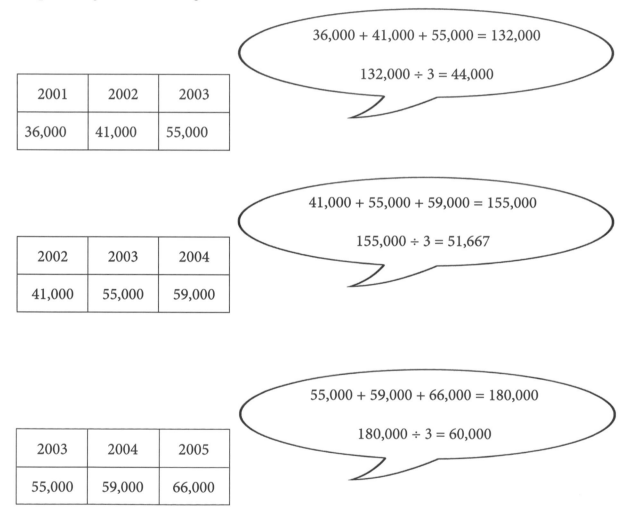

2001	2002	2003
36,000	41,000	55,000

36,000 + 41,000 + 55,000 = 132,000

132,000 ÷ 3 = 44,000

2002	2003	2004
41,000	55,000	59,000

41,000 + 55,000 + 59,000 = 155,000

155,000 ÷ 3 = 51,667

2003	2004	2005
55,000	59,000	66,000

55,000 + 59,000 + 66,000 = 180,000

180,000 ÷ 3 = 60,000

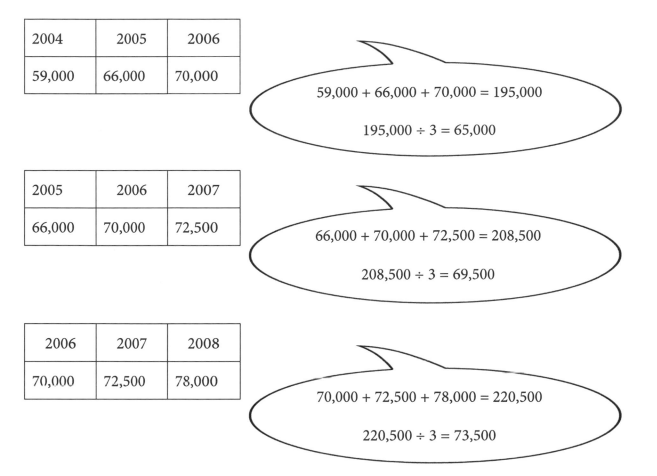

2004	2005	2006
59,000	66,000	70,000

59,000 + 66,000 + 70,000 = 195,000

195,000 ÷ 3 = 65,000

2005	2006	2007
66,000	70,000	72,500

66,000 + 70,000 + 72,500 = 208,500

208,500 ÷ 3 = 69,500

2006	2007	2008
70,000	72,500	78,000

70,000 + 72,500 + 78,000 = 220,500

220,500 ÷ 3 = 73,500

All of the average amounts are then placed into the original table:

Year	2001	2002	2003	2004	2005	2006	2007	2008
Number of people	–	44,000	51,667	60,000	65,000	69,500	73,500	–

Now try these:

1. Find the three point moving average of the following data:

	Monday	Tuesday	Wednesday	Thursday	Friday	Saturday	Sunday
Number of people	34	23	41	22	51	33	48

2. Find the five point moving average of the following data:

	A	B	C	D	E	F	G	H	I
Amount of students	23	13	31	42	26	47	28	19	21

Section 10 - Quadratic Equations

The Fundamentals

A quadratic equation is an equation where the highest power of x is 2. The quadratic could therefore look like any of the following:

The equation may be shown as equal to zero but this is not always the case.

$x^2 - 2x + 3$
$2 + x^2 + 4x = 0$
$5x - 2x^2 + 1$
$9x = x^2 + 6$
$(x + 6)(4x - 5) = 0$

The quadratic equation could also be written in this format and then expanded.

With quadratics, you may be asked to either expand, factorise or solve the equation.

Expand

This means removing the brackets by multiplying them out.

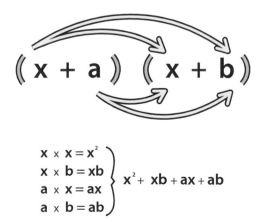

$$\left. \begin{array}{l} x \times x = x^2 \\ x \times b = xb \\ a \times x = ax \\ a \times b = ab \end{array} \right\} \quad x^2 + xb + ax + ab$$

Each arrow represents the parts that need to be multiplied together. You could think of these arrows as creating smiles and frowns. This is where the minus rules are very important as you need to look at each part.

You could also remember this as 'FOIL'. You multiply the first two numbers/unknowns in the brackets, the outside numbers/unknowns, the inside two and finally the last two.

For example:

Expand $(x + 5)(x - 9) = 0$

$x \times x = x^2$
$5 \times x = 5x$
$-9 \times x = -9x$
$5 \times -9 = -45$

An alternative to looking at each arrow in turn is to put the brackets into a grid as shown below. This will ensure that you do not miss any of the parts.

	x	$+5$
x	x^2	$5x$
-9	$-9x$	-45

By writing the answers in a row, you also get $x^2 + 5x - 9x - 45$.

The question is likely to ask you to expand and simplify. This means you need to simplify the line. Remember that the terms cannot all be added together, x^2 and x are completely different, think of the shopping lists in the 'Simplifying Expressions' section.

The only parts that will join together are the $5x$ and $-9x$, these together will therefore be $-4x$ so the expression simplifies to $x^2 - 4x - 45$.

Factorise

Factorising involves putting the brackets back in so you can complete $(x + ?)(x + ?)$.

Think of a quadratic equation as follows $ax^2 + bx + c$. You are looking for two numbers that multiply to give ac and the same two numbers that add together to give b. These two numbers can be slotted into the brackets.

When you have a quadratic that starts with x^2 it means that $a = 1$. You are effectively finding two numbers that multiply to give c, but also multiply together to give b. Always start by looking at how c could be made as there are limited options.

For example:

$x^2 + 8x + 12 = 0$

12 can be made as follows:

1 x 12
2 x 6
4 x 3

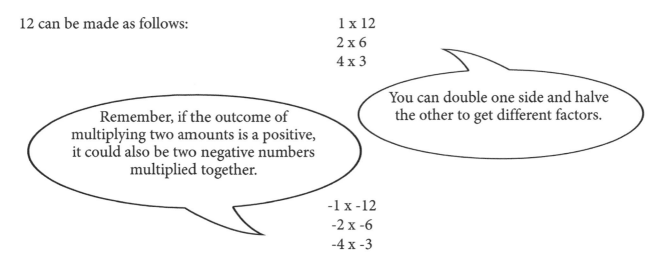

You can double one side and halve the other to get different factors.

Remember, if the outcome of multiplying two amounts is a positive, it could also be two negative numbers multiplied together.

-1 x -12
-2 x -6
-4 x -3

Look through the possible values and add them together to find the following:

1 + 12 = 13
2 + 6 = 8
4 + 3 = 7
-1 + -12 = -13
-2 + -6 = -8
-4 + -3 = -7

The values you need are therefore 6 and 2 so these are replaced into the brackets.

$(x + 6)(x + 2)$

For example:

Factorise $x^2 - 4x - 21 = 0$

-21 can be made as follows:

-1 x 21

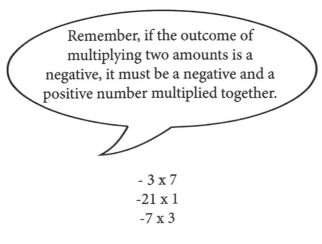

Remember, if the outcome of multiplying two amounts is a negative, it must be a negative and a positive number multiplied together.

- 3 x 7
-21 x 1
-7 x 3

167

Again, look through the possible values and add them together to find the following:

$$-1 + 21 = 20$$
$$-3 + 7 = 4$$
$$-21 + 1 = -20$$
$$-7 + 3 = -4$$

The values you need are therefore -7 and 3 so these are replaced into the brackets. It does not matter which order you put them in the brackets.

$$(x + 3)(x - 7)$$

Solving quadratic equations

You may be asked to solve a quadratic equation, but you would need to factorise the equation first. Once the quadratic equation has been factorised, take the brackets separately and make each one equal zero. This can then be rearranged to get x on its own. You should have two values of x.

For example:

Solve $(x + 6)(x + 2)$

$x + 6 = 0$
$\quad x = 0 - 6$
$\quad x = -6$

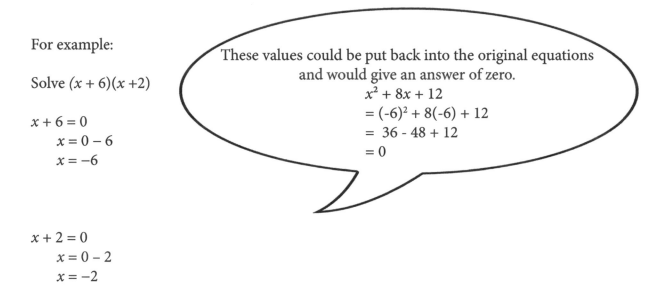

These values could be put back into the original equations and would give an answer of zero.
$$x^2 + 8x + 12$$
$$= (-6)^2 + 8(-6) + 12$$
$$= 36 - 48 + 12$$
$$= 0$$

$x + 2 = 0$
$\quad x = 0 - 2$
$\quad x = -2$

Solve $x^2 - 4x - 21$

You have already seen that this factorises to $(x + 3)(x - 7)$ so you can solve this by splitting the brackets and making them equal zero.

$x + 3 = 0$
    $x = 0 - 3$
    $x = -3$

$x - 7 = 0$
    $x = 0 + 7$
    $x = 7$

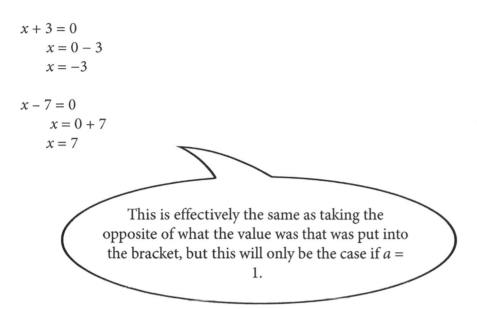

This is effectively the same as taking the opposite of what the value was that was put into the bracket, but this will only be the case if $a = 1$.

Now try these:

1. Expand:

    a) $(5t + 3)(t - 2)$
    b) $(4y - 5)(3y - 7)$
    c) $(r + 8)(r + 6)$

2. Factorise:

    a) $x^2 + 7x + 6$
    b) $y^2 - 9y + 14$
    c) $t^2 + 6t - 16$

3. Solve:

    a) $(x + 5)(x - 9)$
    b) $t^2 - 6t - 16$
    c) $y^2 - 15y + 36$

Quadratic Equations – Higher Level

Factorising

What about if a ≠ 1?

If a does not equal one you need to find the two values that multiply to equal ac, and also add together to make b. The numbers cannot go straight into the brackets as they did previously. Instead b will be replaced by the two numbers and you need to factorise the equation differently.

For example:

$6x^2 - 5x - 4 = 0$

Two numbers that multiply to give -24 (ac) and add together to give -5 (b)

-24 can be made as follows:
- -1 x 24
- - 2 x 12
- -4 x 6
- -8 x 3
- -24 x 1
- -12 x 2
- -6 x 4
- -3 x 8

Look through the possible values and add them together to find the following:

$$-1 + 24 = 23$$
$$- 2 + 12 = 10$$
$$-4 + 6 = 2$$
$$-8 + 3 = -5$$
$$-24 + 1 = -23$$
$$-12 + 2 = -10$$
$$-6 + 4 = -2$$
$$-3 + 8 = 5$$

The two values are therefore -8 and 3 which are replaced into the equation instead of b:

$$6x^2 + 3x - 8x - 4 = 0$$

You can then factorise the equation by splitting it into two, and factorising both parts separately.

$$3x(2x + 1) - 4(2x + 1) = 0$$

Once factorised the brackets should be exactly the same, this can help you work out the second bracket when factorising, but also to check if you are on the right track.

The repeated bracket is one of the correct, but the parts that are currently not in a bracket make up the second bracket.

$$(3x - 4)(2x + 1)$$

Solving when a ≠ 1

As before, once the quadratic equation has been factorised, you need to take the brackets separately and make each one equal zero. This can then be rearranged to get x on its own.

For example:

Solve $(3x - 4)(2x + 1)$

$3x - 4 = 0$
$\quad 3x = 0 + 4$
$\quad 3x = 4$
$\quad x = 4 \div 3$

$\quad x = 1.33 \text{ (2dp)}$

$2x + 1 = 0$
$\quad 2x = 0 - 1$
$\quad 2x = -1$
$\quad x = -1 \div 2$
$\quad x = -0.5$

These values could be put back into the original equations and would give an answer of zero.

$6x^2 - 5x - 4$
$\quad = 6(-0.5)^2 - 5(-0.5) - 4$
$\quad = 1.5 + 2.5 - 4$
$\quad = 0$

Completing the square

Another way of solving quadratics is to 'complete the square'. This means changing the format of the equation but it also gives the two solutions.

$$6x^2 - 5x - 4 = 0$$

In order to complete the square, follow these steps:

<u>Step 1</u>

Make sure the $a = 1$ in the quadratic equation. If there is a number before the x^2 divide the whole equation by the number.

$$x^2 - \frac{5}{6}x - \frac{4}{6} = 0$$

<u>Step 2</u>

Rearrange the quadratic equation so that the unknowns are on one side and the number is on its own on the other side.

$$x^2 - \frac{5}{6}x = \frac{4}{6}$$

<u>Step 3</u>

Take $(\frac{1}{2}b)^2$ and add this to both sides.

$$x^2 - \frac{5}{6}x + \left(\frac{-5}{12}\right)^2 = \frac{4}{6} + \left(\frac{-5}{12}\right)^2$$

The side with the unknowns can now be shown as $(x + \frac{1}{2}b)^2$ as this does give the same answer.

<u>Step 4</u>

Rearrange to get the unknown on its own. The square sign will be the first thing to move to the other side making it a square root.

$$(x - \frac{5}{12})^2 = \frac{4}{6} + \frac{25}{144}$$

$$x - \frac{5}{12} = \pm\sqrt{\frac{121}{144}}$$

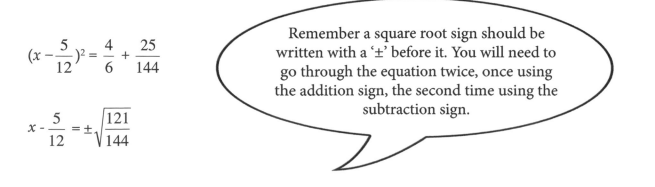

Remember a square root sign should be written with a '±' before it. You will need to go through the equation twice, once using the addition sign, the second time using the subtraction sign.

$$x = \pm\sqrt{\frac{121}{144}} + \frac{5}{12}$$

$$x = \pm\frac{11}{12} + \frac{5}{12}$$

$x = -0.5$ and $x = 1.33$ (2dp)

graph.

Quadratic Formula

In addition to the methods shown previously, you can also use the quadratic formula to solve the quadratic equations. You need to replace the values of a, b and c into the formula below.

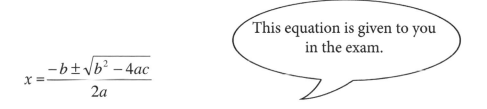

$$x = \frac{-b \pm \sqrt{b^2 - 4ac}}{2a}$$

This equation is given to you in the exam.

For example:

$$6x^2 - 5x - 4 = 0$$

$$a = 6 \quad b = -5 \quad c = -4$$

$$x = \frac{-(-5) \pm \sqrt{(-5)^2 - 4(6)(-4)}}{2(6)}$$

$$x = \frac{5 \pm \sqrt{25 - 4(-24)}}{12}$$

$$x = \frac{5 \pm \sqrt{25 + 96}}{12}$$

$$x = \frac{5 \pm \sqrt{121}}{12}$$

$$x = \frac{5 \pm 11}{12}$$

$$x = \frac{16}{12} \text{ and } x = -\frac{6}{12} \qquad x = 1.33 \text{ and } x = -0.5$$

Now try these:

1. Solve using the quadratic formula:

   a) $3x^2 - 4x - 5$
   b) $2x^2 + 7x - 3$

2. Factorise and solve:

   a) $12x^2 + 17x - 5$
   b) $8x^2 - 18x + 9$

3. Solve, by completing the square, $2x^2 + 10x + 12 = 0$

Areas using Quadratic Equations

The exam paper may test quadratics equations whilst also testing areas.

This could be done by giving the lengths of a rectangle as algebraic expressions instead of numbers. You would then need to multiply the two lengths together which is effectively expanding the brackets.

For example:

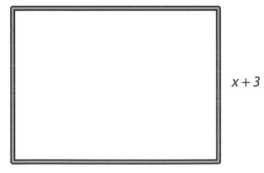

$2x + 1$

$(2x + 1)(x + 3)$
$= 2x^2 + x + 6x + 3$
$= 2x^2 + 7x + 3$

In addition you may be told what the actual area is so that you can find the values of x by working backwards.

For example:

Find y if the area of a rectangle below is 105cm[2].

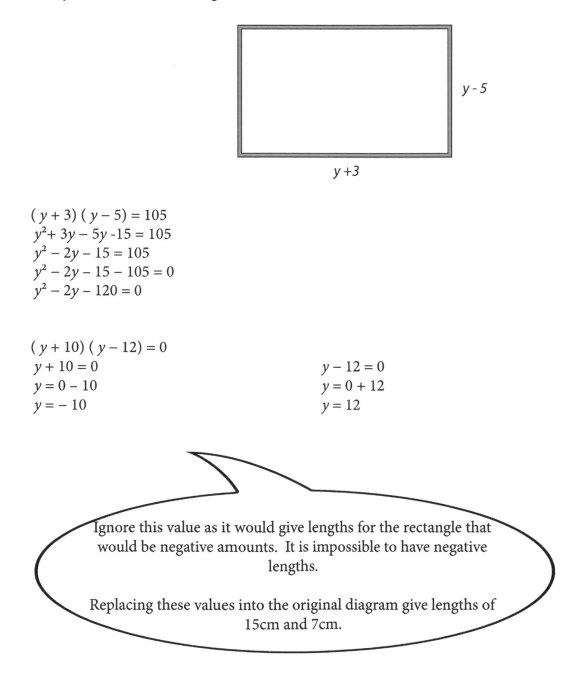

$y - 5$

$y + 3$

$(y + 3)(y - 5) = 105$
$y^2 + 3y - 5y - 15 = 105$
$y^2 - 2y - 15 = 105$
$y^2 - 2y - 15 - 105 = 0$
$y^2 - 2y - 120 = 0$

$(y + 10)(y - 12) = 0$

$y + 10 = 0$ $y - 12 = 0$
$y = 0 - 10$ $y = 0 + 12$
$y = -10$ $y = 12$

Ignore this value as it would give lengths for the rectangle that would be negative amounts. It is impossible to have negative lengths.

Replacing these values into the original diagram give lengths of 15cm and 7cm.

Now try these:

1. Find an expression to represent the area of the rectangle below:

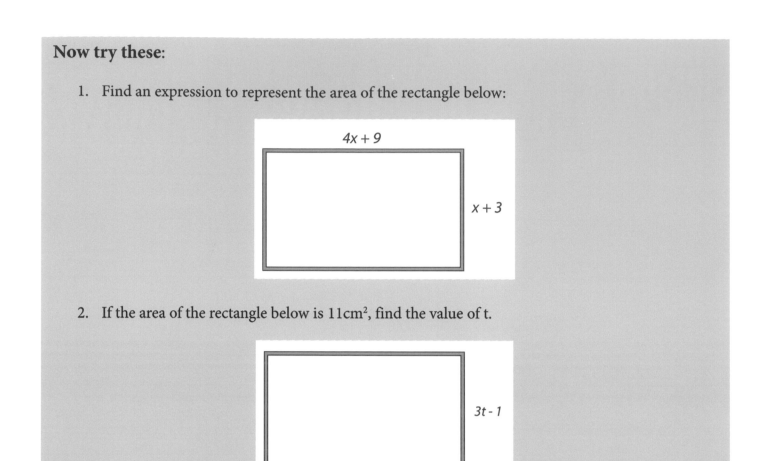

2. If the area of the rectangle below is 11cm², find the value of t.

Quadratic Graphs

The graph of a quadratic equation is called the parabola which is a curve. If the quadratic equation is positive, the graph will be in the shape of a smile. If the equation is a negative, the graph will be in the shape of a frown.

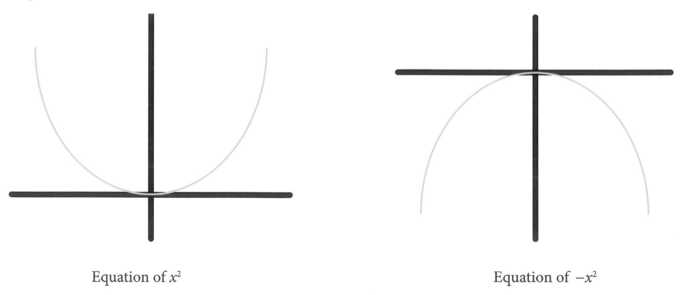

Equation of x^2 Equation of $-x^2$

The two points found to be x, are the two points where the parabola crosses the x axis. The point where it crosses the y axis is the point where $x = 0$.

You may be asked to sketch a graph for an equation.

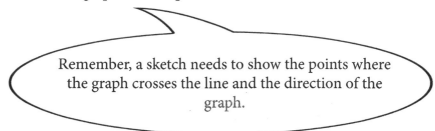

Remember, a sketch needs to show the points where the graph crosses the line and the direction of the graph.

For example:

Sketch graph of $x^2 - 4x - 21$

As shown earlier in the book you can factorise this equation to get $(x - 7)(x + 3)$. This solves to give $x = 7$ and $x = -3$.

This equation will represent a positive parabola as the equation is positive. It will cross the x axis at points $x = 7$ and $x = -3$ as shown below. It will cross the y axis at $y = -21$.

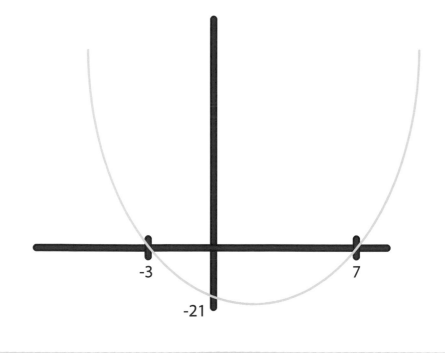

Now try these:

1. Sketch the graph $x^2 + 7x - 18$

2. Sketch the graph $-x^2 - x + 6$

Section 11 – Further Algebra

Simultaneous Equations

Simultaneous equations are two equations with two unknowns. There are many possible answers that fit into the equations but only one set of values that fit into both equations. To show this, if you drew the graphs they would only cross once.

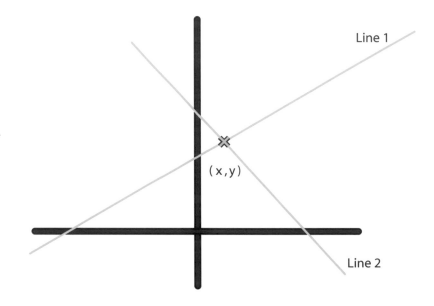

Linear Equations

It is possible to look at the equations below and work out the missing values but you would only receive the answer mark for the question. You also need to show your workings to gain the method marks.

$$2x + y = 9$$
$$3y - 7 = -x$$

Follow these steps in order to solve the equations:

<u>Step 1</u>
Make sure that the unknown letters are in the same columns.

The equations need to be rearranged using skills shown in the algebra section to ensure there is an 'x column', a 'y column' and the numbers are in the same column. The equation would therefore change to the following:

$$2x + y = 9$$
$$x + 3y = 7$$

Make sure that there is the same amount of either x or y. In the above example this is the case, but if it was not you would need to multiply either one or both lines by numbers that would produce the same amount of one of the unknowns.

$$2x + y = 9$$
$$x + 3y = 7$$

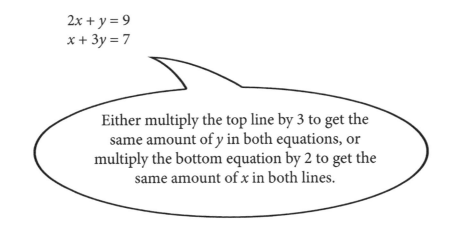

Either multiply the top line by 3 to get the same amount of y in both equations, or multiply the bottom equation by 2 to get the same amount of x in both lines.

If you multiply the bottom line by 2 you will have:

$$2x + \ y = 9$$
$$2x + 6y = 14$$

Step 3
As there is the same amount either x or y, either add or take the lines away from each other. You need to do the one which would get rid of the unknown that you have the same amount of. The action that would get rid of one of the unknowns needs to be applied to every column as shown below.

$$2x \ + \ y \ = 9$$
$$- \quad - \quad \quad -$$
$$2x \ + 6y = 14$$
$$0 - 5y \ = -5$$
$$y \ = -5 \div -5$$
$$y = 1$$

Step 4
Once you know one of the unknowns, you can put this back into one of the original equations. It will work in either of the equations but the original equations will have smaller numbers. The equation can then be rearranged to get the second unknown on its own.

$$2x + y \ = 9$$
$$2x + 1 = 9$$
$$2x = 9 - 1$$
$$2x = 8$$
$$x = 8 \div 2$$
$$x = 4$$

You can check your answer by putting the two values you find back into the original equation.

$$2x + y = 9$$
$$3y - 7 = -x$$
$$x = 4 \quad y = 1$$
$$2(4) + 1 = 9$$
$$3(1) - 7 = -4$$

The values work in both equations.

Linear and Quadratic Equations

If you are given two simultaneous equations where one is a linear equation and the other is a quadratic equation the method will be different.

There will always be two values of x and y when you have a quadratic and a linear equation. This is because the two graphs would cross twice as shown below:

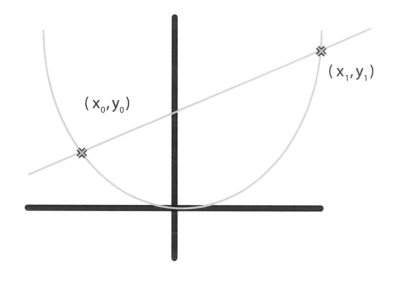

For example:

$$y - x = 4$$
$$2x^2 + xy + y^2 = 8$$

You need to substitute the linear equation into the quadratic equation by rearranging the linear equation to be either x or y.

$$y = 4 + x$$

The '4 + x' can then be replaced into the quadratic equation where there is a value of y.

$$2x^2 + x(4 + x) + (4 + x)^2 = 8$$

The brackets can then be expanded and the equation simplified.

$$2x^2 + 4x + x^2 + 16 + 8x + x^2 = 8$$
$$4x^2 + 12x + 8 = 0$$

This can then be factorised following normal factorising rules once it has all been divided by 4.

$$x^2 + 3x + 2 = 0$$
$$(x + 2)(x + 1) = 0$$

$$x + 2 = 0 \qquad x + 1 = 0$$
$$x = -2 \qquad\quad x = -1$$

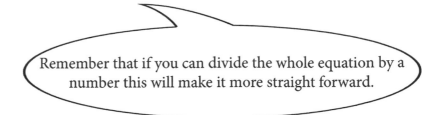

Remember that if you can divide the whole equation by a number this will make it more straight forward.

Once you have the values for x you can then find the values of y for each of the x values.

When $x = -2$

$$y = 4 + x$$
$$y = 4 - 2$$
$$y = 2$$

When $x = -1$

$$y = 4 + x$$
$$y = 4 - 1$$
$$y = 3$$

Now try these:

1. Solve the simultaneous equations

$$2x + 7 = 5y$$
$$3x - 2y = 6$$

2. Solve the simultaneous equations

$$x + 4y = 7$$
$$2x + 3y = 9$$

3. Solve the simultaneous equations

$$y + 2 = x$$
$$x^2 + y^2 = 34$$

Standard Form

Standard form can be used to write very large or very small numbers.

The general template for this is a x 10^n where a is a number between 1 and 10.

Finding numbers from standard form:

Where n is positive, the number will be larger than 1 and 'n' shows how many figures should follow where the point is. If there are not enough numbers shown you need to make up the remaining amount with zeros.

For example:

4.56 x $10^5 = 456,000$
5.3 x $10^4 = 53,000$
2.746 x $10^3 = 2,746$

> You need five numbers after the four. There are only 2 figures there so you need to make the rest up with zeros.

Where n is negative, the number will be a decimal and n tells you how many zeros go in front of the number, including the one before the decimal point.

For example:

3.456 x $10^{-3} = 0.003456$
5.46 x $10^{-5} = 0.0000546$
1.001 x $10^{-2} = 0.01001$

Putting the numbers into standard form:

If the number is not a decimal write out the first part of the number as a decimal between 1 and 10. You can then count how many figures follow the point and put this number above the 10.

For example:

$37,000 = 3.7$ x 10^4

If the number is a decimal write the figures that follow the zeros as a decimal between 1 and 10. You can then count the zeros that are before the figures, this is the number written above 10 as a negative.

For example:

$0.003001 = 3.001 \times 10^{-3}$

Multiplication and division of standard form

When you multiply or divide standard form it is very similar to the index rules.

For example:

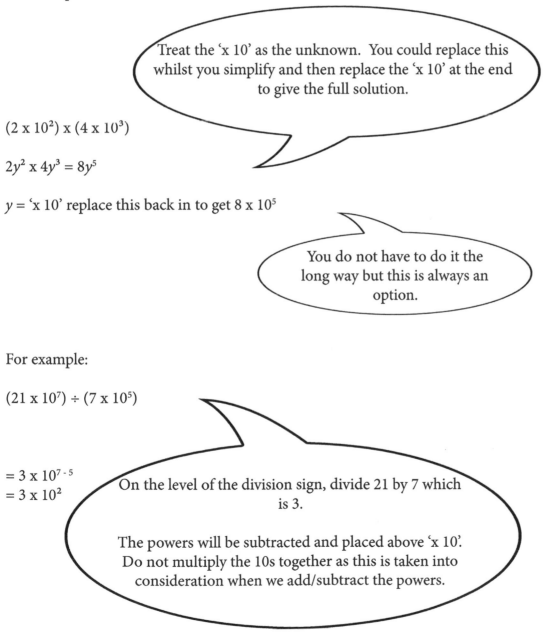

$(2 \times 10^2) \times (4 \times 10^3)$

$2y^2 \times 4y^3 = 8y^5$

$y = $ 'x 10' replace this back in to get 8×10^5

Treat the 'x 10' as the unknown. You could replace this whilst you simplify and then replace the 'x 10' at the end to give the full solution.

You do not have to do it the long way but this is always an option.

For example:

$(21 \times 10^7) \div (7 \times 10^5)$

$= 3 \times 10^{7-5}$
$= 3 \times 10^2$

On the level of the division sign, divide 21 by 7 which is 3.

The powers will be subtracted and placed above 'x 10'. Do not multiply the 10s together as this is taken into consideration when we add/subtract the powers.

Now try these:

1. Write the following in standard form:
a) 498, 000
b) 0.00750034
c) 54,200
d) 0.1000354
e) 6,870
f) 4,765,001

2. Work out:
a) 3.76×10^{-7}
b) 4.817×10^{4}
c) 9.007×10^{6}
d) 3.12×10^{-3}
e) 5.3002×10^{3}
f) 3.000×10^{5}

3. Work out:
a) $(3 \times 10^{8}) \times (7 \times 10^{2})$
b) $(36 \times 10^{5}) \div (9 \times 10^{3})$
c) $(4 \times 10) \times (5 \times 10^{6})$
d) $(24 \times 10^{11}) \div (8 \times 10^{4})$

Rearranging Equations

You have already seen how to solve equations, the method is exactly the same if rearranging equations. The main difference is that you will not get an actual value as the solution, there will be unknowns within the answer.

For example:

Rearrange to get y on its own:

$$x = \frac{y+3}{7}$$

$7x = y + 3$

$7x - 3 = y$

If the unknown you are trying to get on its own appears more than once but cannot be simplified by using the 'who ate all the pies' rule, there is a different method to follow.

For example:

Rearrange to get y on its own:

$$xy = yt + 3$$

Get the unknown that you want on its own all on one side.

$$xy - yt = 3$$

You can then insert a bracket with the unknown on the outside which means it will only appear once.

$$y(x - t) = 3$$

You can then move the bracket to the other side leaving y on its own.

$$y = \frac{3}{(x-t)}$$

Now try these:

1. Rearrange the following equation to get x on its own:

$$yx = 2x + 3$$

2. Rearrange the following equation to get r on its own:

$$xr + rt = 4$$

Trial and Improvement

These are very easy questions and worth lots of marks. You will need to insert values into equations to find the most accurate value.

For example:

$$x^3 + 2x = 15 \qquad \text{find } x \text{ to } 1dp$$

Start by finding which two whole numbers the solution lies between:

$x = 2$ $2^3 + (2 \times 2) = 8 + 4 = 12$ Too low
$x = 3$ $3^3 + (2 \times 3) = 27 + 6 = 33$ Too high

You can see the solution is between 2 and 3

If you inserted values higher than $x = 3$ you are only going to get even higher results.

Now let's try with 1dp

           $x = 2.5$ $2.5^3 + (2 \times 2.5) = 20.625$ Too high
Go lower: $x = 2.2$ $2.2^3 + (2 \times 2.2) = 15.048$ Too high
Go lower: $x = 2.1$ $2.1^3 + (2 \times 2.1) = 13.461$ Too low

You can see the number must lie between 2.1 and 2.2.

If you need to find the answer to 1dp, look at which answer is the closest.

If you are asked to find the answer to 2dp, you know it is between 2.1 and 2.2.
$x = 2.15$ $2.15^3 + (2 \times 2.15) = 14.238\ldots$ Too low
$x = 2.16$ $2.16^3 + (2 \times 2.16) = 14.397\ldots$ Too low
$x = 2.19$ $2.19^3 + (2 \times 2.19) = 14.88\ldots$ Too low

So again, we need to find the closest number:

When $x = 2.19$ Answer = 14.88…   0.12 away
When $x = 2.20$ Answer = 15.048…   0.048 away

Therefore the answer is $x = 2.20$ (to 2dp).

1. Find x to 1dp if $x^3 + 4x = 34$ if x lies between 2 and 3.

2. Find x to 1dp if $x^3 + 3x = 6$ if x lies between 1 and 2.

3. Find x to 2dp if $x^3 - 9x = 73$ if x lies between 4 and 5.

Proportion

Proportion questions either refer to direct proportion or inverse proportion. You need to translate the questions into Maths.

Direct proportion

Direct proportion is the direct effect two variables can have on each other. If one increases, so will the other and vice versa if one decreases.

For example, if x is proportional to y then you would replace the 'proportional to' with ' $= k$'.

This then becomes $x = ky$

You should read the question and translate into this format.

For example:

If w is proportional to v^2, find the value of k when $w = 54$ and $v = 3$.

$w = kv^2$
$54 = 3^2 k$
$54 = 9k$
$k = 54 \div 9$
$k = 6$

Inverse proportion

Inverse proportion has an indirect effect between two variables. As one variable increases, the other decreases and vice versa.

For example, if x is inversely proportional to y then you would replace the 'inversely proportional' with '$= 1/k$'.

This then becomes $x = \dfrac{y}{k}$.

For example:

If t is inversely proportional to the square root of r, find the value of k when $t = 2$ and $r = 36$.

$$t = \frac{\sqrt{r}}{k}$$

$$2 = \frac{\sqrt{36}}{k}$$

$$2 = \frac{6}{k}$$

$$2k = 6$$

$$k = 6 \div 2$$

$$k = 3$$

Now try these:

1. Given that a is directly proportional to b^4 when $a = 48$ and $b = 2$, find the value of k and the value of a when $b = 3$.

2. Given that c is inversely proportional to the cube root of d when $c = 16$ and $d = 64$, find the value of k and the value of c when $d = 125$.

Surds

A surd is a number which is left in the format of a square root. It is left as a square root as it cannot be written as an integer.

For example:

$\sqrt{5}$ is a surd as the actual value of this figure is 2.236067 (6dp). Do not round this figure as the answer would be inaccurate therefore it is left in the square root.

You would not write $\sqrt{9}$ as a surd as the actual value would be 3. It does not therefore need to be left within the square root sign.

Multiplying Surds

When multiplying surds, the two surds need to come together to make one large surd.

For example:
$$\sqrt{5} \times \sqrt{8} = \sqrt{5 \times 8} = \sqrt{40}$$

If you multiply the two numbers together it makes a square number you can then take the square root to get an integer.

For example:
$$\sqrt{12} \times \sqrt{3} = \sqrt{12 \times 3} = \sqrt{36} = 6$$

If this is not the case, look for factors of the new number that are also square numbers. You can then split the surd back into two surds but preferably using square numbers where possible.

For example:
$$\sqrt{8} \times \sqrt{10} = \sqrt{80}$$
$$\sqrt{80} = \sqrt{16} \times \sqrt{5} = 4\sqrt{5}$$

Even if you did not pick a square number first, you would still get down to the same answer but not as quickly so try to think ahead.

Rationalising the denominator

A rational number is a number that can be expressed as an integer or a fraction. If this is not the case, the number is irrational and would be written as a surd.

If there is a fraction which has a surd on the bottom, this can be rationalised. You do this by multiplying the top and bottom of the fraction by the 'opposite' of the bottom. By 'opposite' you need to change the sign in the middle.

If the denominator is $(1 + \sqrt{2})$ multiply both the top and bottom of the fraction by $(1 - \sqrt{2})$.

For example:

Rationalise the denominator of $\dfrac{1}{1+\sqrt{2}}$

$$\dfrac{1}{1+\sqrt{2}} \times \dfrac{1-\sqrt{2}}{1-\sqrt{2}}$$

$$= \dfrac{1(1-\sqrt{2})}{(1+\sqrt{2})(1-\sqrt{2})}$$

$$= \dfrac{1-\sqrt{2}}{1+\sqrt{2}-\sqrt{2}-2}$$

$$= \dfrac{1-\sqrt{2}}{1-2}$$

$$= \dfrac{1-\sqrt{2}}{-1}$$

$$= \sqrt{2}-1$$

Now try these:

1. Simplify $\sqrt{8} \times \sqrt{12}$

2. Rationalise the denominator:

    a) $\dfrac{8}{5-\sqrt{3}}$

    b) $\dfrac{2+\sqrt{5}}{\sqrt{2}-1}$

3. Simplify $\sqrt{108}$

Solutions

Section 1

Terminology

1. 96   1
    48   2
    24   4
    12   8
    6   16
    3   32

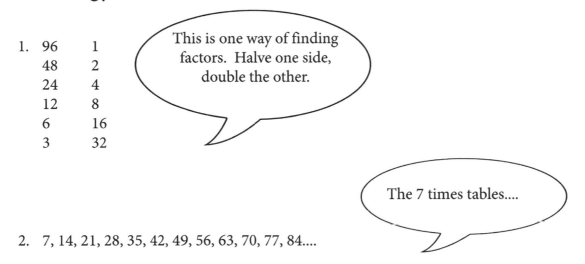

This is one way of finding factors. Halve one side, double the other.

The 7 times tables....

2. 7, 14, 21, 28, 35, 42, 49, 56, 63, 70, 77, 84....

3.

Factors of 18		Factors of 54	
18	1	54	1
9	2	27	2
6	3	18	3
		9	6

The highest common factor is therefore 18.

4.

Factors of 33		Factors of 18	
33	1	18	1
11	3	9	2
		6	3

The highest common factor is therefore 3.

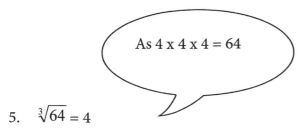

As 4 x 4 x 4 = 64

5. $\sqrt[3]{64} = 4$

6. $2^5 = 2 \times 2 \times 2 \times 2 \times 2 = 32$

Negative Numbers

1. $-4 \times 7 = -28$

2. $50 \div -5 = -10$

Do the numbers first, then look at the signs.

3. $16 + (-19) = 16 - 19 = -3$

4. $5 - (-8) = 5 -- 8 = 5 + 8 = 13$

Rounding

1. a) 23.613 (3dp)
   b) 2.051 (3dp)
   c) 8.610 3dp)

The 9 becomes a 10 so this rounds up to 8.610

2. a) 0.000299 (3sf)
   b) 89,800 (3sf)
   c) 85.4 (3sf)

Estimations

1. $\dfrac{23 \times 6{,}453}{31}$

   $= \dfrac{20 \times 6{,}000}{30}$

Remember, multiply the first numbers then add the same number of zeros to the result.

   $= \dfrac{120{,}000}{30}$

   $= 12{,}000 \div 3 = 4000$

Remember, for every one zero on the top, one zero on the bottom of the fraction can be cancelled out.

2. $\dfrac{2{,}877 \times 62}{12}$

   $= \dfrac{3{,}000 \times 60}{10}$

Remember, for every one zero on the top, one zero on the bottom of the fraction can be cancelled out.

   $= \dfrac{180{,}000}{10}$

   $= 18{,}000 \div 1 = 18{,}000$

3. $\dfrac{324 \times 979}{0.23}$

$= \dfrac{300 \times 1{,}000}{0.2}$

$= 300{,}000 \div 0.2$

$= 300{,}000 \times \dfrac{10}{2}$

$= 1{,}500{,}000$

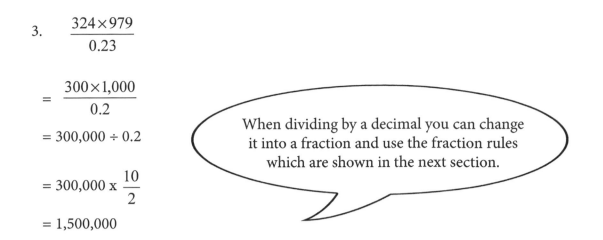

When dividing by a decimal you can change it into a fraction and use the fraction rules which are shown in the next section.

Simplifying Expressions

1. a) $5x + 7y - 3y + x$
   $= 5x + x + 7y - 3y$
   $= 6x + 4y$

   b) $t^2 + 6t + 5t^2 - 2t$
   $= t^2 + 5t^2 - 2t + 6t$
   $= 6t^2 + 4t$

   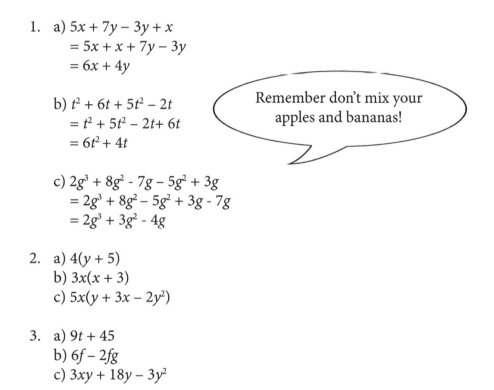

   Remember don't mix your apples and bananas!

   c) $2g^3 + 8g^2 - 7g - 5g^2 + 3g$
   $= 2g^3 + 8g^2 - 5g^2 + 3g - 7g$
   $= 2g^3 + 3g^2 - 4g$

2. a) $4(y + 5)$
   b) $3x(x + 3)$
   c) $5x(y + 3x - 2y^2)$

3. a) $9t + 45$
   b) $6f - 2fg$
   c) $3xy + 18y - 3y^2$

Solving Equations

1. $5x + 3 = 28$
   $5x = 28 - 3$
   $5x = 25$
   $x = 25 \div 5$
   $x = 5$

   Remember the order!

2. $7y - 9 = 3y + 27$

$\qquad 7y = 3y + 27 + 9$

$\quad 7y - 3y = 27 + 9$

$\qquad 4y = 36$

$\qquad\quad y = 36 \div 4$

$\qquad\quad y = 9$

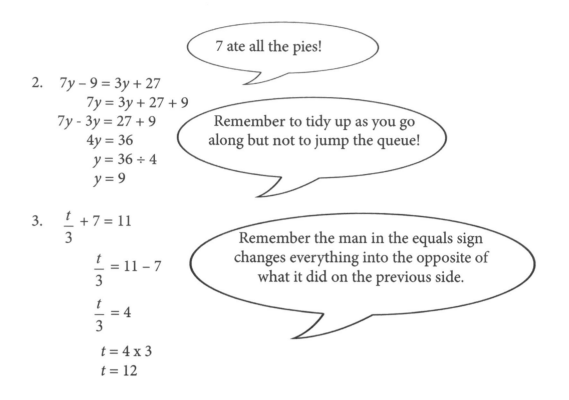

7 ate all the pies!

Remember to tidy up as you go along but not to jump the queue!

Remember the man in the equals sign changes everything into the opposite of what it did on the previous side.

3. $\dfrac{t}{3} + 7 = 11$

$\qquad \dfrac{t}{3} = 11 - 7$

$\qquad \dfrac{t}{3} = 4$

$\qquad t = 4 \times 3$

$\qquad t = 12$

Indices

1. a) $t^5 \times t^7$

$\quad = t^{5+7} = t^{12}$

b) $x^{10} \div x^6$

$\quad = x^{10-6} = x^4$

Remember depending on the level depends on what you will do to the numbers.

c) $g^8 \times g$

$\quad = g^8 \times g^1$

$\quad = g^{8+1} = g^9$

2. a) $6k^2 \times 5k^9$

$\quad = (6 \times 5)k^{2+9} = 30k^{11}$

b) $32f^8 \div 4f$

$\quad = (32 \div 4)f^{8-1} = 8f^7$

The multiply goes up in the air, twists to become a plus. The divide goes up in the air and loses its dots.

c) $7r^3 \times 3r^6$

$\quad = (7 \times 3)r^{3+6} = 21r^9$

Inequalities

1. $8x - 9 \geq 23$
    $8x \geq 23 + 9$
    $8x \geq 32$
    $x \geq 32 \div 8$
    $x \geq 4$

If there are two sides remember to move the number to both sides. This is why the 7 goes to both sides.

2. $-3 < 5x + 7 \leq 22$
    $-3 - 7 < \quad 5x \quad \leq 22 - 7$
    $-10 < \quad 5x \quad \leq 15$
    $10 \div 5 < \quad x \quad \leq 15 \div 5$
    $-2 < \quad x \quad \leq 3$

3. $6x - 11 \geq 2x + 13$
    $6x - 2x \geq 13 + 11$
    $4x \geq 24$
    $x \geq 24 \div 4$
    $x \geq 6$

Remember that the inequality will flip round the opposite way if you multiply or divide by a negative.

4. $12 - 8x \geq 60$
    $-8x \geq 60 - 12$
    $-8x \geq 48$
    $x \leq 48 \div -8$
    $x \leq -6$

Section 2
Fractions

1. $\dfrac{7}{11} \div \dfrac{3}{8} = \dfrac{7}{11} \times \dfrac{8}{3} = \dfrac{56}{33} = 1\dfrac{23}{33}$

Remember you always multiply to find the answer with all fractions.

2. $\dfrac{6}{7} + \dfrac{9}{10} = \dfrac{60 + 63}{70} = \dfrac{123}{70} = 1\dfrac{53}{70}$

3. $\dfrac{11}{12} - \dfrac{4}{5} = \dfrac{55 - 48}{60} = \dfrac{7}{60}$

4. $5\dfrac{1}{2} - 1\dfrac{4}{5} = \dfrac{11}{2} - \dfrac{9}{5} = \dfrac{55 - 18}{10} = \dfrac{37}{10} = 3\dfrac{7}{10}$

5. $2\dfrac{1}{4} + 3\dfrac{2}{3} = \dfrac{9}{4} + \dfrac{11}{3} = \dfrac{27 + 44}{12} = \dfrac{71}{12} = 5\dfrac{11}{12}$

Finding a Percentage

1. £600 x 10% = £60
           5% = £30
          2.5% = £15
       17.5% = £105

    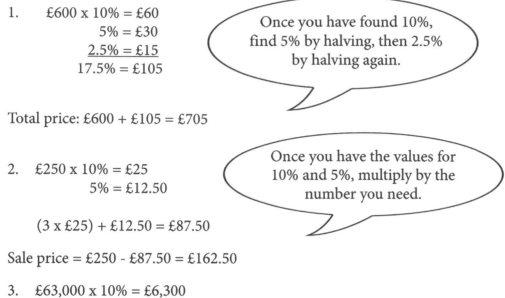

    Once you have found 10%, find 5% by halving, then 2.5% by halving again.

Total price: £600 + £105 = £705

2. £250 x 10% = £25
          5% = £12.50

    Once you have the values for 10% and 5%, multiply by the number you need.

    (3 x £25) + £12.50 = £87.50

Sale price = £250 - £87.50 = £162.50

3. £63,000 x 10% = £6,300
            1% = £630
    (2 x £6,300) + (4 x £630) = £15,120

Changing Percentage, Decimals and Fractions

1. a) $43\% = \dfrac{43}{100}$

    b) $0.71 = 71\% = \dfrac{71}{100}$

    c) $0.01 = 1\% = \dfrac{1}{100}$

    d) $20\% = \dfrac{20}{100} = \dfrac{1}{5}$

2. a) $5\% = 0.05$

    b) $\dfrac{3}{8} = \dfrac{1}{8} \times 3 = 0.125 \times 3 = 0.375$

    c) $23\% = 0.23$

    Remember to use the H.T.U template for changing between decimals and percentages.

    d) $\dfrac{13}{20} \times 5 = \dfrac{65}{100} = 0.65$

3. a) $0.91 = 91\%$

    b) $\dfrac{7}{10} = \dfrac{70}{100} = 70\%$

    c) $0.03 = 3\%$

    d) $\dfrac{3}{5} = \dfrac{60}{100} = 60\%$

Remember to make the denominator of the fraction 100 as you can then read the top figure as the percentage.

Recurring Decimals

1. $100x = 582.\overset{..}{8}\overset{}{2}$

    $99x = 582.\overset{..}{8}\overset{}{2} - 5.\overset{..}{8}\overset{}{2}$

    $99x = 577$

    $x = \dfrac{577}{99}$

    $x = 5\dfrac{82}{99}$

Two figures are repeated which is why you multiply by 100 and the fraction denominator is 99.

2. $1000x = 124.\overset{...}{1}\overset{}{2}\overset{}{4}$

    $999x = 124.\overset{...}{1}24 - 0.\overset{...}{1}24$

    $999x = 124$

    $x = \dfrac{124}{999}$

Three figures are repeated which is why you multiply by 1000 originally and the fraction denominator is 999.

Percentage Change

Remember the famous yellow cartoon character!

1. Difference = 16 (40 - 24)
    Original value = 40

    $\dfrac{16}{40} \times 100\%$

    = 40% decrease

2. Difference = £150 (£350 - £200)
    Original value = £200

    $\dfrac{150}{200} \times 100\%$

    = 75% increase

Compound Interest

1. 1 January 2005 = £300
    1 January 2006 = £300 x 1.06 = £318.00
    1 January 2007 = £318 x 1.06 = £337.08

2. End of Year 1 = £150,000 x 1.05 = £157,500.00
    End of Year 2 = £157,500 x 1.05 = £165,375.00
    End of Year 3 = £165,375 x 1.05 = £173,643.75

3. End of Year 1 = £240.00 x 1.08 = £259.20
    End of Year 2 = £259.20 x 1.08 = £279.94
    End of Year 3 = £279.94 x 1.08 = £302.34
    End of Year 4 = £302.34 x 1.08 = £326.53

Finding Original Values

Divide by 7 to get 10%, then multiply by 10 to get 100%.

1. 70% = £245

    10% = £35

    Original Value = £350

Divide by 12 to get 10%, then multiply by 10 to get 100%.

2. 120% = £144,000

    10% = £12,000

    Original Value = £120,000

Divide by 8.5 to get 10%, then multiply by 10 to get 100%.

3. 85% = £59.50

    10% = £7

    Original Value = £70

Check this by making sure these values equal the original 132.

Ratios

1. 1 + 2 + 4 + 5 = 12
    132 ÷ 12 = 11

    Annie: 1 x 11 = 11 sweets   Tasha: 2 x 11 = 22 sweets
    Cerian: 4 x 11 = 44 sweets   Heidi: 5 x 11 = 55 sweets

2. 2 + 3 + 4 = 9
    £1800 ÷ 9 = £200

    Helen: 2 x £200 = £400   Sean: 3 x £200 = £600   Kerry: 4 x £200 = £800

3. $3 + 4 = 7$
   $63 \div 7 = 9$

Juliet: $3 \times 9 = 27$ Linda: $4 \times 9 = 36$

Probability

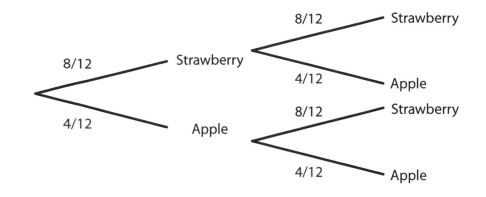

1.

Strawberry 'and' Strawberry

$$\frac{8}{12} \times \frac{8}{12} = \frac{64}{144} = \frac{4}{9} \text{ (divide both top and bottom by 16)}$$

Strawberry 'and' Apple

$$\frac{8}{12} \times \frac{4}{12} = \frac{32}{144} = \frac{2}{9} \text{ (divide both top and bottom by 16)}$$

Apple 'and' Strawberry

$$\frac{4}{12} \times \frac{8}{12} = \frac{32}{144} = \frac{2}{9} \text{ (divide both top and bottom by 16)}$$

Apple 'and' Apple

$$\frac{4}{12} \times \frac{4}{12} = \frac{16}{144} = \frac{1}{9} \text{ (divide both top and bottom by 16)}$$

2. Probability of Ace 'and' Probability of Ace

$$\frac{4}{52} \times \frac{3}{51} = \frac{12}{2652} = \frac{1}{221}$$

3. $1 - 0.32 = 0.68$

Section 3

Areas and Volumes of Shapes

1.   ½ x (3 + 7) x 5
   = ½ x 10 x 5
   = 25 cm²

Remember, the 6 is not required.

2. a) Area of circle = π x 6² = 113.09733......
       Volume of cylinder = 113.09733....... x 11cm
                   = 1244.07 cm³ (2dp)

Remember, this is not the end of the question don't round yet.

  b) Volume of sphere = $\frac{4}{3}$ x π x 7³ = 1436.76 cm³ (2dp)

Areas and Volumes with algebra

1.

	$\dfrac{4rst}{3\pi}$	$\dfrac{4t^2s}{3r} + \dfrac{3s^3}{2r}$	$2\pi r^2$	$\dfrac{3r^2s^3t}{st^2}$	$4rt^2 + \dfrac{3s^2r}{2}$
Area/Volume?	Volume	Area	Area	Volume	Volume

2.

$7mp + 7n^2$	$\dfrac{pn^2}{7m} + \dfrac{6p^3}{m^2\pi}$	$5\pi pmn$	$\dfrac{6pm^2}{n\pi} + \dfrac{n^2p}{m^2}$
Area	Area + Length	Volume	Area + Length

Circles

1. If diameter is 7cm, radius = 3.5cm.
   Area = π x 3.5² = 38.48 cm² (2dp)

2. If radius is 5cm, diameter = 10cm.
   Circumference = π x 10 = 31.416 cm (3dp)

3. Area of circle = π x 5² = 78. 5398...... cm²
   Area of rectangle = 8 x 6 = 48 cm²
   Shaded area = 78.5398.....cm² – 48cm²
               = 30.540 cm² (3dp)

Sectors & Segments

1. $\pi \times 8^2 \times \dfrac{230}{360}$

   $= 128.\,46 \text{ cm}^2 \text{ (2dp)}$

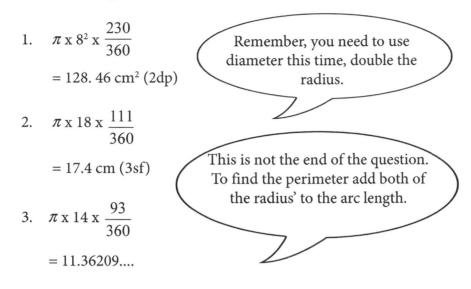

2. $\pi \times 18 \times \dfrac{111}{360}$

   $= 17.4 \text{ cm (3sf)}$

3. $\pi \times 14 \times \dfrac{93}{360}$

   $= 11.36209....$

   $11.36209... + 7\text{cm} + 7\text{cm} = 25.36 \text{ cm (2dp)}$

4. Area of sector:

   $$\pi \times 7^2 \times \dfrac{150}{360} = 64.1408..... \text{ cm}^2$$

   Area of the triangle:

   $$\tfrac{1}{2} \times 7\text{cm} \times 7\text{cm} \times \text{Sin } 150° = 12.25 \text{ cm}^2$$

   Area of segment: $64.1408... - 12.25 = 51.89 \text{ cm}^2 \text{ (2dp)}$

Section 4

Triangles

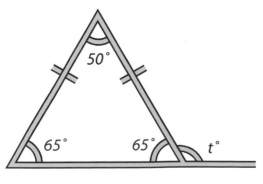

1.

The triangle is an isosceles triangle so the bottom angles will be 65° as shown.

Using the angles on a straight line rule, $65° + t = 180°$ so $t = 115°$.

2. The triangle is an isosceles triangle so the two unknown lengths will be the same.

$$x + x + 3\text{cm} = 21\text{cm}$$
$$2x + 3\text{cm} = 21\text{cm}$$
$$2x = 18\text{cm}$$
$$x = 9\text{cm}$$

Pythagorus Theorem

1. $\sqrt{11^2 - 6^2}$

    $= \sqrt{121 - 36}$

    $= \sqrt{85}$

    $= 9.220\text{cm (3dp)}$

    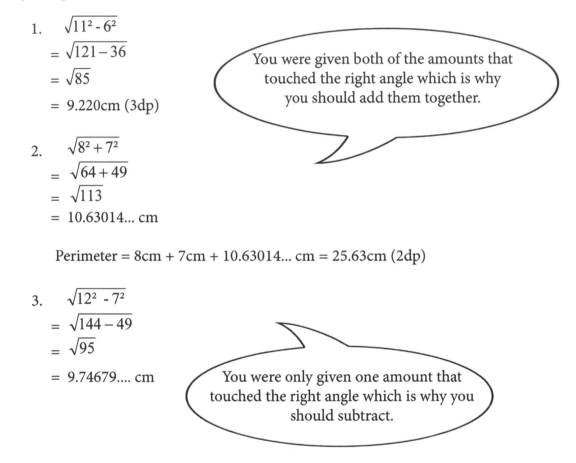

    You were given both of the amounts that touched the right angle which is why you should add them together.

2. $\sqrt{8^2 + 7^2}$

    $= \sqrt{64 + 49}$

    $= \sqrt{113}$

    $= 10.63014...\text{ cm}$

    Perimeter $= 8\text{cm} + 7\text{cm} + 10.63014...\text{ cm} = 25.63\text{cm (2dp)}$

3. $\sqrt{12^2 - 7^2}$

    $= \sqrt{144 - 49}$

    $= \sqrt{95}$

    $= 9.74679....\text{ cm}$

    You were only given one amount that touched the right angle which is why you should subtract.

    Area $= ½ \times 9.74679... \times 7 = 34.11\text{ cm}^2\text{ (2dp)}$

Trigonometry

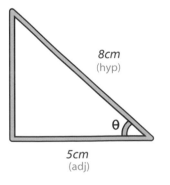

8cm
(hyp)

θ

5cm
(adj)

1.

$$\text{Cos } \theta = \frac{5}{8} \qquad \qquad \theta = 51.32° \text{ (2dp)}$$

2.

$$\text{Sin } 47 = \frac{7}{y}$$

$$\text{Sin } 47 \text{ x } y = 7$$

$$y = 7 \div \text{Sin } 47$$

$$y = 9.57\text{cm (2dp)}$$

3.

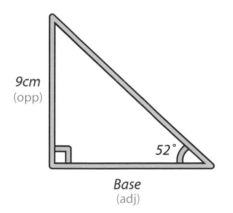

$$\text{Tan } 52 = \frac{9}{x}$$

$$\text{Tan } 52 \text{ x } x = 9$$

$$x = 9 \div \text{Tan } 52$$

$$x = 7.0315706..... \text{ cm}$$

Area = ½ x 9 x 7.0315706..... = 31.642 cm² (3dp)

Similar Triangles

1. Scale factor = 3.5
   $r = 21 \div 3.5 = 6$cm
   $t = 6 \times 3.5 = 21$cm

The triangles are similar so one is an enlargement of the other. If a length of 4cm becomes 14cm, there is a scale factor of 3.5.

2. Scale factor = 3
   $f = 18 \div 3 = 6$cm
   $g = 5 \times 3 = 15$cm

If a length of 4cm becomes 12cm, there is a scale factor of 3.

Sine & Cosine Rule

1. $\dfrac{Sin\theta}{9} = \dfrac{Sin98}{14}$

   $Sin\,\Theta = \dfrac{Sin98}{14} \times 9$

   $Sin\,\Theta = 0.6366009.....$
   $\Theta = 39.54°$ (2dp)

Remember, always change the formula to have the unknown on the top of the fraction.

2. $\dfrac{y}{Sin38} = \dfrac{12}{Sin69}$

   $y = \dfrac{12}{Sin69} \times Sin\,38$

   $y = 7.91$cm (2dp)

Remember, when you have a complete pair and will have two complete pairs by the end of the question, use the sine rule.

3. $Cos\,A = \dfrac{b^2 + c^2 - a^2}{2bc}$

   $Cos\,\Theta = \dfrac{8^2 + 7^2 - 14^2}{2(8)(7)}$

   $Cos\,\Theta = \dfrac{64 + 49 - 196}{112}$

There is no right angle, and no complete pair but you are finding an angle. You therefore need to use the cosine rule but remember to rearrange it.

$$\text{Cos}\,\Theta = \frac{-83}{112}$$

$$\Theta = 137.82 \text{ (2dp)}$$

4. ½ x 10 x 12 x *Sin* 61
    = 52.477cm² (3dp)

You need to find the area of the triangle but you do not have the base and height. You also have an angle which prompts you to use the formula.

5. ½ x 11 x 9 x Sin 123
    = 41.514cm² (3dp)

Section 5

Sequences

1.

n	1	2	3	4	5
Un	6	13	20	27	34
a		7	7	7	7

When $n = 1$, $Un = 6$, when $n = 2$, $Un = 13$, when $n = 3$, $Un = 20$, etc.

$a = 7$

$$Un = an + b$$
$$6 = 7(1) + b$$
$$6 = 7 + b$$
$$6 - 7 = b$$
$$b = -1$$

$$13 = 7(2) + b$$
$$13 = 14 + b$$
$$13 - 14 = b$$
$$b = -1$$

The constant is the same so proves this is correct.

$$Un = 7n - 1$$
$$Un = 7(50) - 1$$
$$Un = 350 - 1$$
$$Un = 349$$

2.

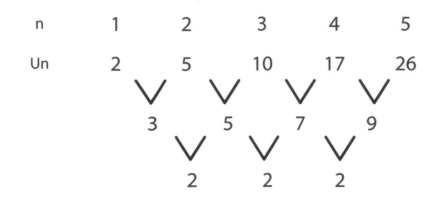

When $n = 1$, $Un = 2$, when $n = 2$, $Un = 5$, when $n = 3$, $Un = 10$, etc.

$Un = n^2 + b$
$2 = (1)^2 + b$
$2 = 1 + b$
$2 - 1 = b$
$b = 1$

$5 = (2)^2 + b$
$5 = 4 + b$
$5 - 4 = b$
$b = 1$

The constant is the same so proves this is correct.

$Un = n^2 + 1$
$Un = (85)^2 + 1$
$Un = 7225 + 1$
$Un = 7226$

3.

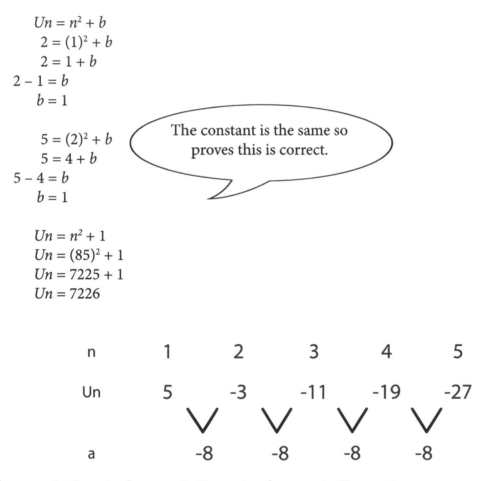

When $n = 1$, $Un = 5$, when $n = 2$, $Un = -3$, when $n = 3$, $Un = -11$, etc.

$a = -8$

$Un = an + b$
$5 = -8(1) + b$
$5 = -8 + b$
$5 + 8 = b$
$b = 13$

$$-3 = -8(2) + b$$
$$-3 = -16 + b$$
$$-3 + 16 = b$$
$$b = 13$$

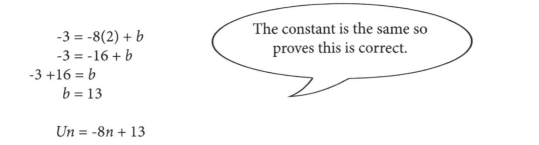
The constant is the same so proves this is correct.

$$Un = -8n + 13$$

Distance, Speed & Time

1. $9\text{km/hr} \times \dfrac{2}{3}\ \text{hr} = 6\ \text{km}$

2. $150\ \text{miles} \div 3\ \text{hours} = 50\ \text{miles per hour}$

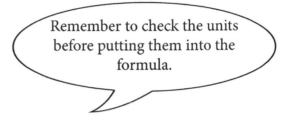
Remember to check the units before putting them into the formula.

3. $\dfrac{1}{3}\ \text{hr} \times 24\text{km/hr} = 8\text{km}$

4. The person travels 2km at a constant speed for 1½ hours. They rest for 1 hour then the last 3km in ½ hour.

Mass, Density & Volume

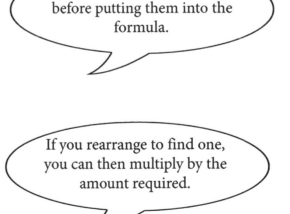
Remember to check the units before putting them into the formula.

1. $500\text{g} \div 25\text{cm}^3 = 20\text{g/cm}^3$

2. $1000\text{g} \div 25\text{g/cm}^3 = 40\text{cm}^3$

Conversions

If you rearrange to find one, you can then multiply by the amount required.

1. $1€ = \dfrac{£1}{1.20}$

   $465€ = \dfrac{£1}{1.20} \times 465 = £387.50$

2. 1.5kg tomatoes ÷ 6 = 0.25kg x 9 = 2.25kg
   1.2 litres of boiling water ÷ 6 = 0.2 litres x 9 = 1.8 litres
   2 tsp of tomato puree ÷ 6 = 1/3 tsp x 9 = 3 tsp
   2 stock cubes ÷ 6 = 1/3 stock cubes x 9 = 3 stock cubes

3. $2 \times 1.75 = 3.5$ pints

4. £450 = 167 shares

$$\frac{£450}{167} = 1 \text{ share}$$

$$\frac{£450}{167} \times 100 = 100 \text{ shares}$$

£269.46 = 100 shares

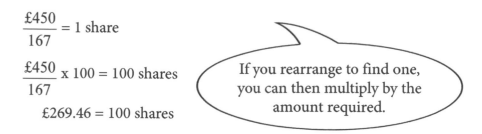

If you rearrange to find one, you can then multiply by the amount required.

Section 6

Angles

1. This is a corresponding angle so $a = 50°$

2. This is an alternate angle as the b is within a 'z' so $b = 75°$

3. $r + 95° = 360°$
   $r = 360° - 95°$
   $r = 265°$

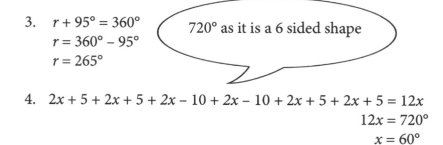

720° as it is a 6 sided shape

4. $2x + 5 + 2x + 5 + 2x - 10 + 2x - 10 + 2x + 5 + 2x + 5 = 12x$
   $$12x = 720°$$
   $$x = 60°$$

Angle Properties of Circles

1. $y = ½$ of $160°$
   $y = 80°$

2. $t + 75° = 180°$
   $t = 180° - 75°$
   $t = 105°$

Transformations

1. Rotation 180° clockwise at (0,0).

2. This is a translation of shape C by (-5, -3).

Symmetry

1. Order of 4:

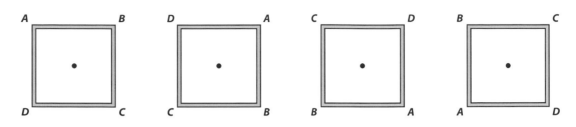

2. 4 lines of symmetry

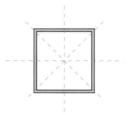

3. 2 lines of symmetry

Bearings

1. 115° - 120°

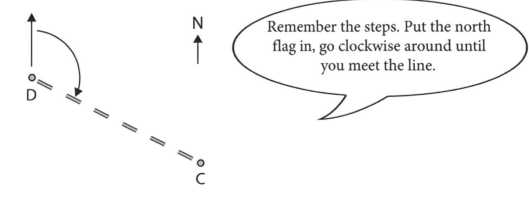

Remember the steps. Put the north flag in, go clockwise around until you meet the line.

2. 265°

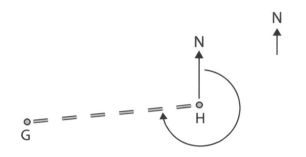

Loci

1.

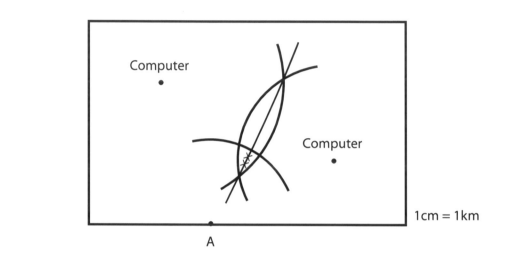

1cm = 1km

2.

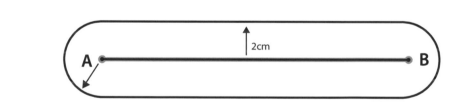

Vectors

1. a) $g - h = e$
   b) $d + b = a$
   c) $f + b = c$
   d) $a - d = b$

Section 7

Graphs

1. (-2, -3) (3 , 5)
2.

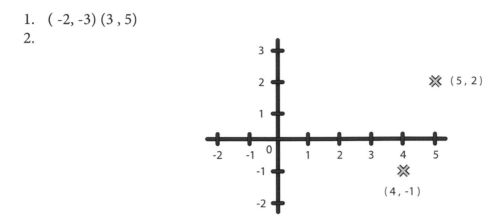

Linear Equations- Straight line graphs

1. $c = 6$

    $y = mx + 6$

    Coordinates $(4 , 0)$

    $0 = 4m + 6$
    $- 6 = 4m$
    $1.5 = m$

    $y = -1.5x + 6$

2. $y = \dfrac{-10}{4} x + \dfrac{8}{4}$

    $y = -2.5x + 2$

    $c = 2$ and putting $y = 0$ into the equation, you get $x = 0.8$.

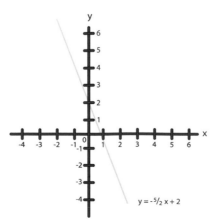

Scatter Graphs

1.

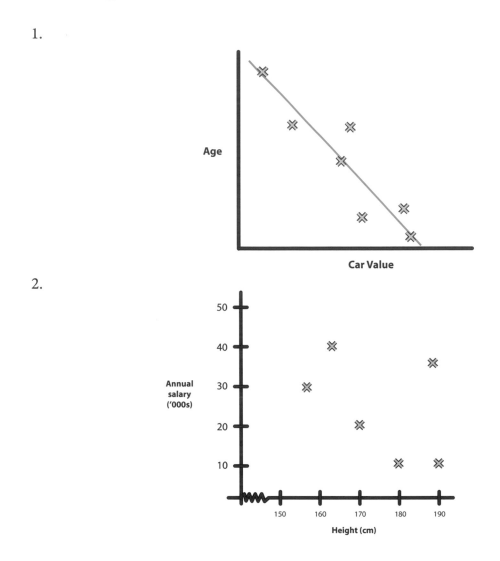

2.

3.   Q1 – Negative correlation
     Q2 – No correlation

Solving equations using graphs

1.

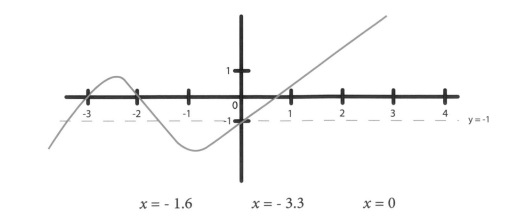

$x = -1.6$ $x = -3.3$ $x = 0$

2.

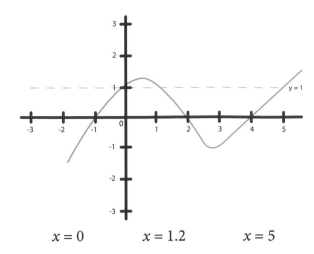

$x = 0$ $x = 1.2$ $x = 5$

Graph Transformations

1. a)

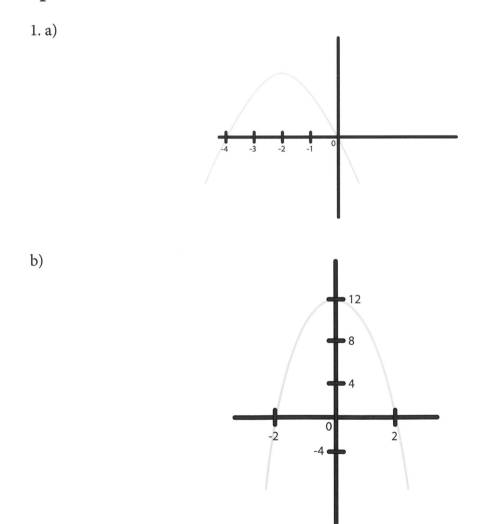

b)

213

Sine, Cosine and Tangent Graphs

1.

    a)   Cos -90° = 0

    b)   Sin 270° = -1

You can read the values off when you do a sketch.

2.

    a)

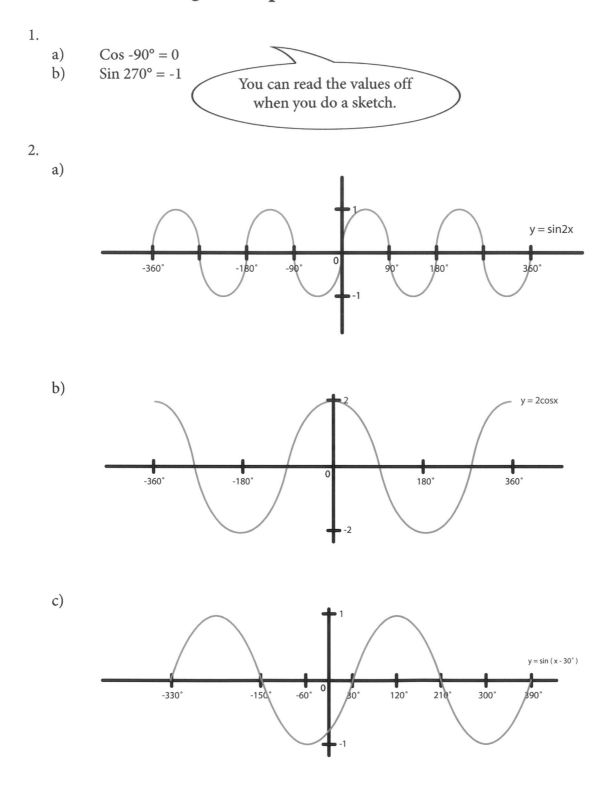

    b)

    c)

Section 8

Collecting Data

1.

Journey to Work	Tally	Frequency
Car	JHT JHT JHT	15
Train	JHT II	7
Bus	JHT JHT	10
Walk	IIII	4
Other	JHT JHT I	11

Representing Data

1. Spain = 18 people
    France = 15 people
    Florida = 30 people
    Mexico = 24 people
    Egypt = 36 people
    Other = 18 people

2. Mode: 37
    Median: ~~12, 13, 14, 26,~~ 29, ~~31, 34, 37, 37~~
    Median: 29
    Range: 37 − 12 = 25

3. Key: 3 │ 4 = 34

3	4	4	5	9
4	1	6		
5	6			
6	4	8		
7	2	6		

215

4.

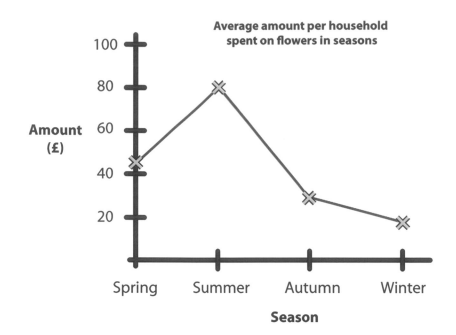

Average amount per household
spent on flowers in seasons

Amount (£): 100, 80, 60, 40, 20

Season: Spring, Summer, Autumn, Winter

Pie charts

1.

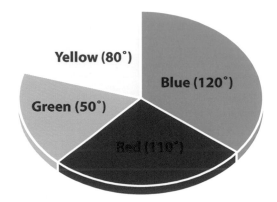

Yellow (80°)

Blue (120°)

Green (50°)

Red (110°)

2.

Type of pet	Frequency	Degrees in sector
Dogs	14	?/36 x 360° = 140°
Cats	7	?/36 x 360° = 70°
Fish	5	?/36 x 360° = 50°
Rabbits	10	?/36 x 360° = 100°
	36	360°

Histograms

1.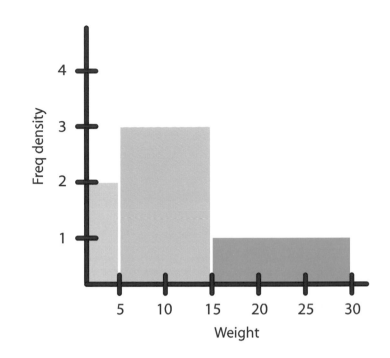

Scores	Frequency	Class Width	Frequency Density
$0 \le x \le 5$	10	5	2
$5 < x \le 15$	30	10	3
$15 < x \le 30$	15	15	1

2.

Scores	Frequency	Class Width	Frequency Density
$0 \le x \le 20$	0.5 x 20 = 10	20	0.5
$20 < x \le 30$	2.5 x 10 = 25	10	2.5
$30 < x \le 50$	1.5 x 20 = 30	20	1.5

Frequency Polygons

1.

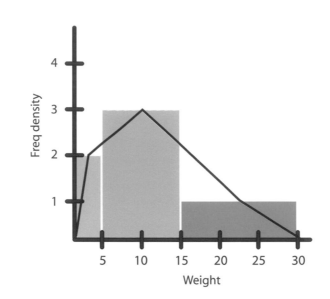

2.

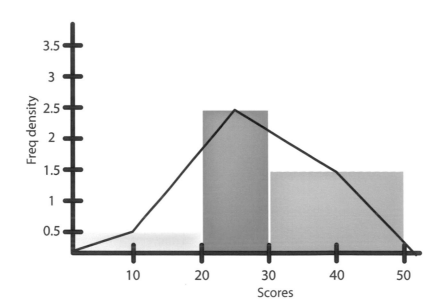

Section 9

Mean, Mode and Median – Single Data

1. Mean: $4 + 9 + 6 + 7 + 5 + 4 + 2 + 1 + 3 + 8 = 49$
   $$49 \div 10 = 4.90$$
   Mode: 4 (appears the most)

   Median: 1, 2, 3, 4, 4, 5, 6, 7, 8, 9
   $$4 + 5 = 9 \div 2 = 4.5$$
   Range: $9 - 1 = 8$

2. Mean: $56 + 98 + 76 + 34 + 61 + 32 + 98 + 65 + 45 + 43 + 11 + 98 = 717$
   $$717 \div 12 = 59.75$$
   Mode: 98 (appears the most)

   Median: 11, 32, 34, 43, 45, 56, 61, 65, 76, 98, 98, 98
   $$56 + 61 = 117 \div 2 = 58.5$$
   Range: $98 - 11 = 87$

Cumulative Frequency

1.

Scores	Frequency	Cumulative Frequency
$0 \le x \le 10$	5	5
$10 < x \le 20$	5	10
$20 < x \le 30$	15	25
$30 < x \le 40$	5	30
Total	30	

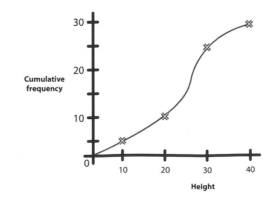

2.

Scores	Frequency	Cumulative Frequency
$0 \leq x \leq 5$	10	10
$5 < x \leq 15$	5	15
$15 < x \leq 20$	10	25
$20 < x \leq 30$	5	30
Total	30	

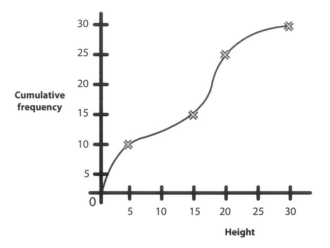

Median and Interquartile Range

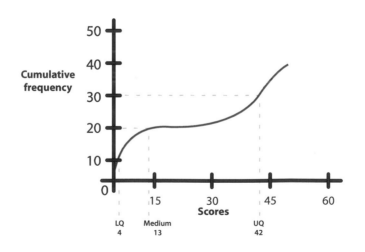

1.

$$IR = 42 - 4 = 38$$

2. Upper quartile – Lower quartile = Interquartile Range

        50   –   25   =   25

Box Plots

1.

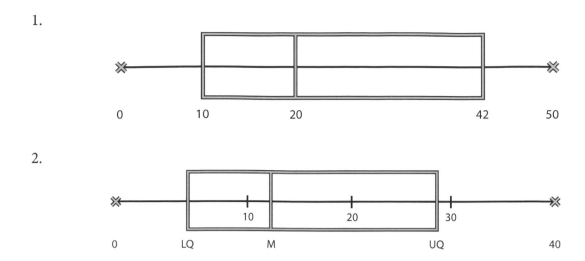

2.

Moving Average

1.

Monday	Tuesday	Wednesday
34	23	41

34 + 23 + 41 = 98

98 ÷ 3 = 32.67 (2dp)

Tuesday	Wednesday	Thursday
23	41	22

23 + 41 + 22 = 86

86 ÷ 3 = 28.67 (2dp)

Wednesday	Thursday	Friday
41	22	51

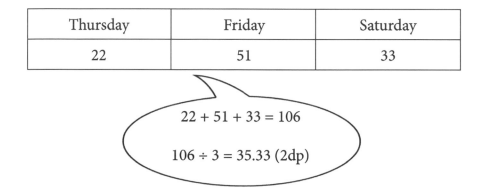

41 + 22 + 51 = 114

114 ÷ 3 = 38

Thursday	Friday	Saturday
22	51	33

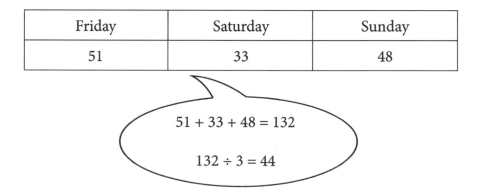

22 + 51 + 33 = 106

106 ÷ 3 = 35.33 (2dp)

Friday	Saturday	Sunday
51	33	48

51 + 33 + 48 = 132

132 ÷ 3 = 44

All of the average amounts are then placed into the original table:

	Monday	Tuesday	Wednesday	Thursday	Friday	Saturday	Sunday
Number of people	-	32.67	28.67	38	35.33	44	-

2.

A	B	C	D	E
23	13	31	42	26

23 + 13 + 31 + 42 + 26 = 135

135 ÷ 5 = 27

B	C	D	E	F
13	31	42	26	47

13 + 31 + 42 + 26 + 47 = 159

159 ÷ 5 = 31.8

C	D	E	F	G
31	42	26	47	28

31 + 42 + 26 + 47 + 28 = 174

174 ÷ 5 = 34.8

D	E	F	G	H
42	26	47	28	19

42 + 26 + 47 + 28 + 19 = 162

162 ÷ 5 = 32.4

E	F	G	H	I
26	47	28	19	21

$26 + 47 + 28 + 19 + 21 = 141$

$141 \div 5 = 28.2$

All of the average amounts are then placed into the original table:

	A	B	C	D	E	F	G	H	I
Amount of students	-	-	27	31.8	34.8	32.4	28.2	-	-

Section 10

Quadratic Equations

1. a) $5t^2 + 3t - 10t - 6$
      $5t^2 - 7t - 6$
   b) $12y^2 - 15y - 28y + 35$
      $12y^2 - 43y + 35$
   c) $r^2 + 8r + 6r + 48$
      $r^2 + 14r + 48$

Remember to expand the brackets using FOIL.
First, Outside, Inside and Last.

2. a) $(x + 1)(x + 6)$
   b) $(y - 7)(y - 2)$
   c) $(t + 8)(t - 2)$

Remember, when $a = 1$ you are looking for two values that multiply to give c and add to give b.

5. Solve:
   a) $x = -5$ $x = 9$
   b) $t = 8$ $t = -2$
   c) $y = 12$ $y = 3$

Remember, you need to factorise before you can solve.

Quadratic Equations – Higher Level

1. a) $3x^2 - 4x - 5$

    $a = 3 \quad b = -4 \quad c = -5$

    $$x = \frac{-(-4) \pm \sqrt{(-4)^2 - 4(3)(-5)}}{2(3)}$$

    $$x = \frac{4 \pm \sqrt{4^2 - 4(-15)}}{6}$$

    $$x = \frac{4 \pm \sqrt{16 + 60}}{6}$$

    $$x = \frac{4 \pm \sqrt{76}}{6}$$

    $$x = \frac{4 \pm 8.71779....}{6}$$

    $x = 2.12$ (2dp) and $x = -0.79$ (2dp)

    b) $2x^2 + 7x - 3$

    $a = 2 \quad b = 7 \quad c = -3$

    $$x = \frac{-(7) \pm \sqrt{(7)^2 - 4(2)(-3)}}{2(2)}$$

    $$x = \frac{-7 \pm \sqrt{7^2 - 4(-6)}}{4}$$

    $$x = \frac{-7 \pm \sqrt{49 + 24}}{4}$$

    $$x = \frac{-7 \pm \sqrt{73}}{4}$$

    $$x = \frac{-7 \pm 8.54400374...}{4}$$

    $x = 0.386$ (3dp) and $x = -3.886$ (3dp)

2. Factorise and solve:

a) $12x^2 + 17x - 5$
$12x^2 + 20x - 3x - 5$
$4x(3x + 5) - 1(3x + 5)$
$(4x - 1)(3x + 5)$
$x = 0.25 \quad x = -1.67$ (2dp)

Remember, when solving you should make each bracket equal zero then rearrange to get x on its own.

b) $8x^2 - 18x + 9$
$8x^2 - 12x - 6x + 9$
$4x(2x - 3) - 3(2x - 3)$
$(4x - 3)(2x - 3)$
$x = 0.75 \quad x = 1.5$

3. $2x^2 + 10x + 12 = 0$
$2x^2 + 10x = -12$
$x^2 + 5x = -6$
$x^2 + 5x + 2.5^2 = -6 + 2.5^2$
$(x + 2.5)^2 = -6 + 6.25$
$x + 2.5 = \pm \sqrt{0.25}$
$x = \pm 0.5 - 2.5$
$x = -2 \quad x = -3$

Areas using Quadratic Equations

1. $(4x + 9)(x + 3)$
$4x^2 + 9x + 12x + 27$
$4x^2 + 21x + 27$

2. $(3t - 1)(2t + 1) = 11$
$6t^2 - 2t + 3t - 1 = 11$
$6t^2 + t - 1 = 11$
$6t^2 + t - 1 - 11 = 0$
$6t^2 + t - 12 = 0$
$6t^2 + 9t - 8t - 12 = 0$
$3t(2t + 3) - 4(2t + 3) = 0$
$(3t - 4)(2t + 3) = 0$
$t = 1.33$ (2dp) $\quad t = -1.5$

This value can be ignored as it would create a negative length which impossible.

Quadratic Graphs

1.

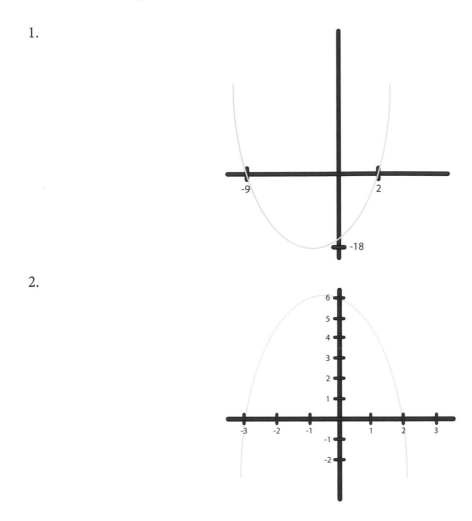

2.

Section 11 – Further Algebra

Simultaneous Equations

1. $2x + 7 = 5y$
    $3x - 2y = 6$
    $2x - 5y = -7$
    $3x - 2y = 6$

    $6x - 15y = -21$
    $6x - 4y = 12$

    $6x - 15y = -21$
    $\underline{6x - 4y = 12}$
    $0 - 11y = -33$
    $\qquad y = -33 \div -11$
    $\qquad y = 3$

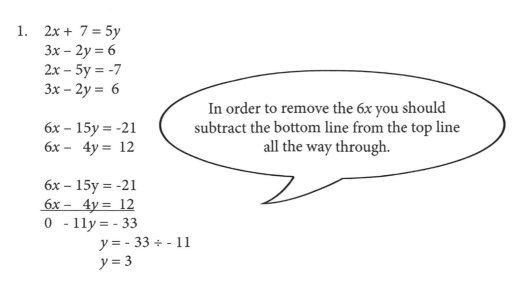

In order to remove the $6x$ you should subtract the bottom line from the top line all the way through.

If $y = 3$:

$$2x + 7 = 15$$
$$2x = 15 - 7$$
$$x = 8 \div 2$$
$$x = 4$$

2. $x + 4y = 7$
    $2x + 3y = 9$

$2x + 8y = 14$
$2x + 3y = 9$

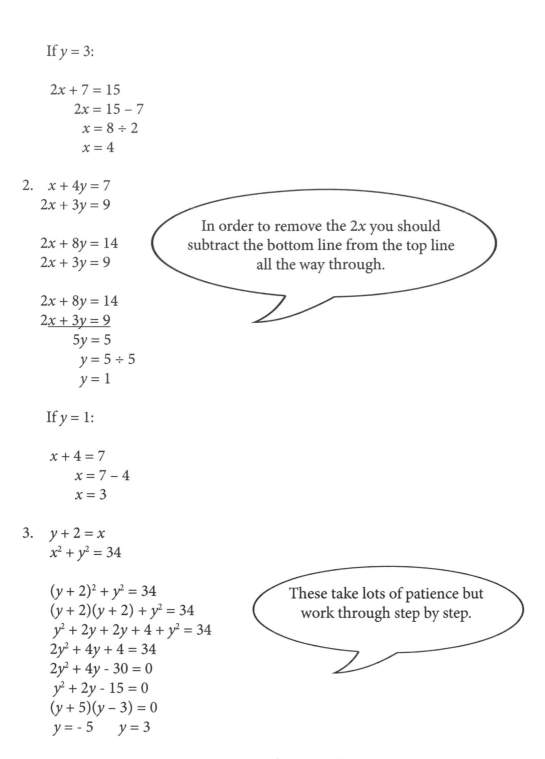

In order to remove the $2x$ you should subtract the bottom line from the top line all the way through.

$2x + 8y = 14$
$\underline{2x + 3y = 9}$
$5y = 5$
$y = 5 \div 5$
$y = 1$

If $y = 1$:

$$x + 4 = 7$$
$$x = 7 - 4$$
$$x = 3$$

3. $y + 2 = x$
    $x^2 + y^2 = 34$

$(y + 2)^2 + y^2 = 34$
$(y + 2)(y + 2) + y^2 = 34$
$y^2 + 2y + 2y + 4 + y^2 = 34$
$2y^2 + 4y + 4 = 34$
$2y^2 + 4y - 30 = 0$
$y^2 + 2y - 15 = 0$
$(y + 5)(y - 3) = 0$
$y = -5 \qquad y = 3$

These take lots of patience but work through step by step.

$y + 2 = x$ So... $x = 5$ when $y = 3$ and $x = -3$ when $y = -5$

Standard Form

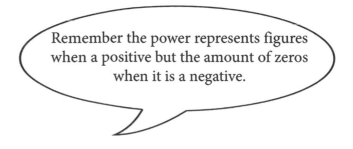

Remember the power represents figures when a positive but the amount of zeros when it is a negative.

1. a) $498,000 = 4.98 \times 10^5$
    b) $0.00750034 = 7.50034 \times 10^{-3}$
    c) $54,200 = 5.42 \times 10^4$
    d) $0.1000354 = 1.000354 \times 10^{-1}$
    e) $6,870 = 6.870 \times 10^3$
    f) $4,765,001 = 4.765001 \times 10^6$

2. a) $3.76 \times 10^{-7} = 0.000000376$
   b) $4.817 \times 10^4 = 48,170$
   c) $9.007 \times 10^6 = 9,007,000$
   d) $3.12 \times 10^{-3} = 0.00312$
   e) $5.3002 \times 10^3 = 5,300.20$
   f) $3.000 \times 10^5 = 300,000$

   > Remember the indice rules from the first section.

3. a) 21×10^{10} or 2.1×10^{11}
   b) 4×10^2
   c) 20×10^7 or 2×10^8
   d) 3×10^7

Rearranging Equations

1. $yx - 2x = 3$
   $x(y - 2) = 3$
   $x = \dfrac{3}{y - 2}$

2. $xr + rt = 4$
   $r(x + t) = 4$
   $r = \dfrac{4}{x + t}$

Trial and Improvement

1. $\quad\quad\quad\quad x = 2.5 \quad 2.5^3 + (4 \times 2.5) = 25.625 \quad\quad$ Too low
   Go higher: $x = 2.8 \quad 2.8^3 + (4 \times 2.8) = 33.152 \quad\quad$ Too low
   Go higher: $x = 2.9 \quad 2.9^3 + (4 \times 2.9) = 35.989 \quad\quad$ Too high

   When $x = 2.8$ $\quad\quad$ Answer $= 33.152$ $\quad\quad$ 0.848 away
   When $x = 2.9$ $\quad\quad$ Answer $= 35.989$ $\quad\quad$ 1.989 away

   Therefore the answer is $x = 2.8$ (to 1dp).

2. $\quad\quad\quad\quad x^3 + 3x = 6$
   $\quad\quad\quad\quad x = 1.5 \quad 1.5^3 + (3 \times 1.5) = 7.875 \quad\quad$ Too high
   Go lower: $x = 1.3 \quad 1.3^3 + (3 \times 1.3) = 6.097 \quad\quad$ Too high
   Go lower: $x = 1.2 \quad 1.2^3 + (3 \times 1.2) = 5.328 \quad\quad$ Too low

   When $x = 1.3$ $\quad\quad$ Answer $= 6.097$ $\quad\quad$ 0.097 away
   When $x = 1.2$ $\quad\quad$ Answer $= 5.328$ $\quad\quad$ 0.672 away

   Therefore the answer is $x = 1.3$ (to 1dp).

3. $x^3 - 9x = 73$

$x = 4.5$	$4.5^3 - (9 \times 4.5) = 50.625$	Too low
Go higher: $x = 4.8$	$4.8^3 - (9 \times 4.8) = 67.392$	Too low
Go higher: $x = 4.9$	$4.9^3 - (9 \times 4.9) = 73.549$	Too high

$x = 4.86$	$4.86^3 - (9 \times 4.86) = 71.0512\ldots$	Too low
$x = 4.88$	$4.88^3 - (9 \times 4.88) = 72.2942\ldots$	Too low
$x = 4.89$	$4.89^3 - (9 \times 4.89) = 72.9201\ldots$	Too low

When $x = 4.89$	Answer = 72.9201…	0.0799…	away
When $x = 4.90$	Answer = 73.549	0.549	away

Therefore the answer is $x = 4.89$ (to 2dp).

Proportion

1. $a = kb^4$
     $48 = k(2)^4$
     $48 = 16k$
      $3 = k$

     If $b = 3$ $a = 3 \times 3^4$
                       $a = 3 \times 81$
                       $a = 243$

2. $c = \dfrac{\sqrt[3]{d}}{k}$

     $16 = \dfrac{\sqrt[3]{64}}{k}$

     $16k = \sqrt[3]{64}$
     $16k = 4$
       $k = 0.25$

     If $d = 125$

     $c = \dfrac{\sqrt[3]{125}}{0.25}$

     $c = 20$

Surds

1. $\sqrt{8} \times \sqrt{12}$

$\quad = \sqrt{8 \times 12}$

$\quad = \sqrt{96}$

$\quad = \sqrt{6 \times 16}$

$\quad = \sqrt{6} \times \sqrt{16}$

$\quad = 4\sqrt{6}$

2. a) $\dfrac{8}{5-\sqrt{3}} \times \dfrac{5+\sqrt{3}}{5+\sqrt{3}}$

$\quad = \dfrac{8(5+\sqrt{3})}{(5-\sqrt{3})(5+\sqrt{3})}$

$\quad = \dfrac{40+8\sqrt{3}}{25-5\sqrt{3}+5\sqrt{3}-3}$

$\quad = \dfrac{40+8\sqrt{3}}{25-3}$

$\quad = \dfrac{40+8\sqrt{3}}{22}$

$\quad = \dfrac{8(5+\sqrt{3})}{22}$

b) $\dfrac{2+\sqrt{5}}{\sqrt{2}-1} \times \dfrac{\sqrt{2}+1}{\sqrt{2}+1}$

$\quad = \dfrac{(2+\sqrt{5})(\sqrt{2}+1)}{(\sqrt{2}-1)(\sqrt{2}+1)}$

$\quad = \dfrac{2\sqrt{2}+\sqrt{10}+2+\sqrt{5}}{2-\sqrt{2}+\sqrt{2}-1}$

$\quad = \dfrac{2\sqrt{2}+\sqrt{10}+2+\sqrt{5}}{2-1}$

$$= \frac{2\sqrt{2} + \sqrt{10} + 2 + \sqrt{5}}{1}$$

$$= 2\sqrt{2} + \sqrt{10} + \sqrt{5} + 2$$

3. $\sqrt{108}$
    $= \sqrt{9 \times 12}$
    $= \sqrt{9} \times \sqrt{12}$
    $= 3 \times \sqrt{4}\,\sqrt{3}$
    $= 3 \times 2\sqrt{3}$
    $= 6\sqrt{3}$

Index

Lightning Source UK Ltd.
Milton Keynes UK
UKIC01n0742151014
240115UK00010B/66